1st EDITION

Perspectives on Modern World History

The Cuban Missile Crisis

1st EDITION

Perspectives on Modern World History

The Cuban Missile Crisis

Myra Immell

Editor

GREENHAVEN PRESS
A part of Gale, Cengage Learning

GALE
CENGAGE Learning

Detroit • New York • San Francisco • New Haven, Conn • Waterville, Maine • London

GALE
CENGAGE Learning·

Christine Nasso, *Publisher*
Elizabeth Des Chenes, *Managing Editor*

© 2011 Greenhaven Press, a part of Gale, Cengage Learning.

Gale and Greenhaven Press are registered trademarks used herein under license.

For more information, contact:
Greenhaven Press
27500 Drake Rd.
Farmington Hills, MI 48331-3535
Or you can visit our Internet site at gale.cengage.com

For product information and technology assistance, contact us at
Gale Customer Support, 1-800-877-4253.

For permission to use material from this text or product, submit all requests online at
www.cengage.com/permissions.

Further permissions questions can be e-mailed to permissionrequest@cengage.com

Articles in Greenhaven Press anthologies are often edited for length to meet page requirements. In addition, original titles of these works are changed to clearly present the main thesis and to explicitly indicate the author's opinion. Every effort is made to ensure that Greenhaven Press accurately reflects the original intent of the authors. Every effort has been made to trace the owners of copyrighted material.

Cover image Custom Medical Stock Photo, Inc. Reproduced by permission.

LIBRARY OF CONGRESS CATALOGING-IN-PUBLICATION DATA

The Cuban Missile Crisis / Myra Immell, book editor.
    p. cm. -- (Perspectives on modern world history)
   Includes bibliographical references and index.
   ISBN 978-0-7377-5005-8 (hardcover)
  1. Cuban Missile Crisis, 1962--Juvenile literature. I. Immell, Myra.
   E841.C83 2010
   972.9106'4--dc22
                                                        2010011349

Printed in the United States of America
1 2 3 4 5 6 7 14 13 12 11 10

CONTENTS

warned that continued offensive military buildup in Cuba would bring repercussions.

In this 1962 address, the president contends that the United States has proof that the Soviet Union has begun a rapid offensive arms build-up in Cuba. The missile bases will provide a nuclear strike capability against the West.

The U.S. president was in a position to force the Soviets to withdraw their missiles.

CHAPTER **3**   Personal Narratives

FOREWORD

The history of each nation is punctuated by momentous events that represent turning points for that nation, with an impact felt far beyond its borders. These events—displaying the full range of human capabilities, from violence, greed, and ignorance to heroism, courage, and strength—are nearly always complicated and multifaceted. Any student of history faces the challenge of grasping the many strands that constitute such world-changing events as wars, social movements, and environmental disasters. But understanding these significant historic events can be enhanced by exposure to a variety of perspectives, whether of people involved intimately or of ones observing from a distance of miles or years. Understanding can also be increased by learning about the controversies surrounding such events and exploring hot-button issues from multiple angles. Finally, true understanding of important historic events involves knowledge of the events' human impact—of the ways such events affected people in their everyday lives—all over the world.

Perspectives on Modern World History examines global historic events from the twentieth-century onward by presenting analysis and observation from numerous vantage points. Each volume offers high school, early college level, and general interest readers a thematically arranged anthology of previously published materials that address a major historical event, with an emphasis on international coverage. Each volume opens with background information on the event, then presents the controversies surrounding that event, and concludes with first-person narratives from people who lived through the event or were affected by it. By providing primary sources from the time of the event, as well as relevant commentary surrounding the event, this series can be used to inform debate, help develop critical thinking skills, increase global awareness, and enhance an understanding of international perspectives on history.

Material in each volume is selected from a diverse range of sources, including journals, magazines, newspapers, nonfiction books, personal narratives, speeches, congressional testimony, government documents, pamphlets, organization newsletters, and position papers. Articles taken from these sources are carefully edited and introduced to provide context and background. Each volume of Perspectives on Modern World History includes an array of views on events of global significance. Much of the material comes from international sources and from U.S. sources that provide extensive international coverage.

Each volume in the Perspectives on Modern World History series also includes:

- A full-color **world map**, offering context and geographic perspective.
- An annotated **table of contents** that provides a brief summary of each essay in the volume.
- An **introduction** specific to the volume topic.
- For each viewpoint, a brief **introduction** that has notes about the author and source of the viewpoint, and that provides a summary of its main points.
- Full-color **charts**, **graphs**, **maps**, and other visual representations.

- Informational **sidebars** that explore the lives of key individuals, give background on historical events, or explain scientific or technical concepts.
- A **glossary** that defines key terms, as needed.
- A **chronology** of important dates preceding, during, and immediately following the event.
- A **bibliography** of additional books, periodicals, and Web sites for further research.
- A comprehensive **subject index** that offers access to people, places, and events cited in the text.

Perspectives on Modern World History is designed for a broad spectrum of readers who want to learn more about not only history but also current events, political science, government, international relations, and sociology—students doing research for class assignments or debates, teachers and faculty seeking to supplement course materials, and others wanting to improve their understanding of history. Each volume of Perspectives on Modern World History is designed to illuminate a complicated event, to spark debate, and to show the human perspective behind the world's most significant happenings of recent decades.

INTRODUCTION

The historical progression of the Cuban missile crisis was quite straightforward: (1) The Soviet Union, under the leadership of Nikita Khrushchev, placed nuclear missiles in Cuba; (2) U.S. president John F. Kennedy insisted they be removed; (3) They were. But for those involved in and living through the crisis, it was not that simple. For them, it was two unforgettable weeks of tension, suspense, fear, and speculation.

Two meetings of the United Nations Security Council captured worldwide attention. The first of these was held October 23, 1962, the eighth day of the crisis. That morning U.S. ambassador Adlai Stevenson called for an emergency meeting of the Security Council to bring to its attention what he called "a grave threat to the Western Hemisphere and to the peace of the world"—"the transformation of Cuba into a base for offensive weapons of sudden mass destruction." A November 2, 1962, *Time* magazine article titled "The United Nations: Until Hell Freezes Over" described the meeting as "a sparring match in which Russia's vulpine [fox-like] Valerian Zorin and Cuba's bouncy Mario Garcia-Incháustegui tried, with ridicule and invective, to outscore U.S. Ambassador Adlai Stevenson."

During that meeting, Stevenson reported that President Kennedy had announced that to combat the military developments taking place in Cuba, the United States was imposing a strict quarantine on offensive military weapons under shipment to Cuba. Stevenson proclaimed that Cuba had "given the Soviet Union a bridgehead and staging area in this hemisphere" and had "invited an extra-continental, antidemocratic and expansionist Power into the bosom of the American family."

He portrayed Cuba as "an accomplice in the communist enterprise of world domination" and argued that when "with cold deliberation" Cuban leader Fidel Castro turned Cuba over to the Soviet Union for a long-range missile-launching base, he was carrying the "Soviet program for aggression into the heart of the Americas." This, Stevenson declared, was more than the United States was willing to tolerate.

Garcia-Incháustegui denounced the U.S. naval quarantine of Cuba as "an act of war" and spoke out at length against American imperialism and the long-standing U.S. threat to the Cuban people. Cuba, he claimed repeatedly, was acting only in its defense against aggressors. Zorin argued that the naval blockade violated the rules of international conduct and accused the United States of "undisguised piracy." He insisted the U.S. claim that the Soviet Union had set up offensive weapons in Cuba was false. The United States, he said, was "trying to misrepresent the measures taken by the Cuban Government to ensure the defense of Cuba." "The Soviet delegation," he announced, "hereby officially confirms the statements already made by the Soviet Union in this connexion, to the effect that the Soviet Government has never sent and is not now sending offensive weapons of any kind to Cuba." He warned that "The peoples of the world must clearly realize . . . that in openly embarking on this venture the United States of America is taking a step along the road which leads to a thermo-nuclear world war."

The second highly publicized meeting of the United Nations Security Council came two days later, on October 25. The episode has been called one of the memorable moments of the Cuban missile crisis and one of the most dramatic confrontations in the history of the UN Security Council. The main players were Valerian Zorin and Adlai Stevenson. In front of delegates from thirteen nations, Stevenson challenged the Soviet ambassador to admit that his country was installing missiles in Cuba. He did not mince words and kept pushing:

> Mr. Stevenson: But if I understood what you said, you said . . . that today I was defensive because we do not have the evidence to prove our assertions that your Government had installed long-range missiles in Cuba. Well, let me say something to you, Mr. Ambassador: We do have the evidence. We have it, and it is clear and incontrovertible. And let me say something else: Those weapons must be taken out of Cuba. . . .
>
> You, the Soviet Union, have sent these weapons to Cuba. You, the Soviet Union, have upset the balance of power in the world. You, the Soviet Union, have created this new danger—not the United States.
>
> You asked, with a fine show of indignation, why the President did not tell [Soviet minister of foreign affairs] Mr. Gromyko last Thursday about our evidence, at the very time that Mr. Gromyko was blandly denying to the President that the USSR was placing such weapons on sites in the New World. Well, I will tell you why: because we were assembling the evidence—and perhaps it would be instructive to the world to see how far a Soviet official would go in perfidy. Perhaps we wanted to know whether this country faced another example of nuclear deceit like the one a year ago, when in stealth the Soviet Union broke the nuclear test moratorium. And, while we are asking questions, let me ask you why your Government, your Foreign Minister, deliberately, cynically deceived us about the nuclear build-up in Cuba.
>
> Finally, Mr. Zorin, I remind you that the other day you did not deny the existence of these weapons. Instead, we heard that they had suddenly become defensive weapons. But today again—if I heard you correctly—you say that they do not exist, or that we have not proved they exist—and you say this with another fine flood of rhetorical scorn. All right, sir, let me ask

you one simple question: Do you, Ambassador Zorin, deny that the USSR has placed and is placing medium- and intermediate-range missiles and sites in Cuba? Yes or no? Do not wait for the interpretation. Yes or no?

Mr. Zorin: I am not in an American courtroom, sir, and therefore I do not wish to answer a question that is put to me in the fashion in which a prosecutor puts questions. In due course, sir, you will have your reply.

Mr. Stevenson: You are in the courtroom of world opinion right now, and you can answer "Yes" or "No." You have denied that they exist—and I want to know whether I have understood you correctly.

Mr. Zorin: Will you please continue your statement, sir? You will have your answer in due course.

Mr. Stevenson: I am prepared to wait for my answer until Hell freezes over, if that is your decision. I am also prepared to present the evidence in this room.

When Zorin did not answer, Stevenson had an easel set up on which he placed a series of aerial reconnaissance photos that proved there were Soviet missiles in Cuba. The audience was stunned. Dissatisfied with Zorin's response to this, Stevenson pressed on:

I have not had a direct answer to my question. The representative of the Soviet Union said that the official answer of the Soviet Union was the *Tass* statement that the USSR does not need to locate missiles in Cuba. I agree: The USSR does not need to do that. But the question is not whether the USSR needs missiles in Cuba. The question is: Has the USSR missiles in Cuba? And that question remains unanswered. I knew it would remain unanswered.

As to the authenticity of the photographs, about which Mr. Zorin has spoken with such scorn, I wonder if the Soviet Union would ask their Cuban colleagues to permit a United Nations team to go to these sites. If so, Mr. Zorin, I can assure you that we can direct them to the proper places very quickly.

And now I hope that we can get down to business, that we can stop this sparring. We know the facts, Mr. Zorin, and so do you, and we are ready to talk about them. Our job here is not to score debating points: Our job, Mr. Zorin, is to save the peace. If you are ready to try, we are.

Time magazine called Stevenson's presentation, which came to be known as the Adlai Stevenson moment, the "best performance since he took his job at the U.N." It convinced the world that the missiles existed and that the United States was determined to see them removed from Cuba.

World Map

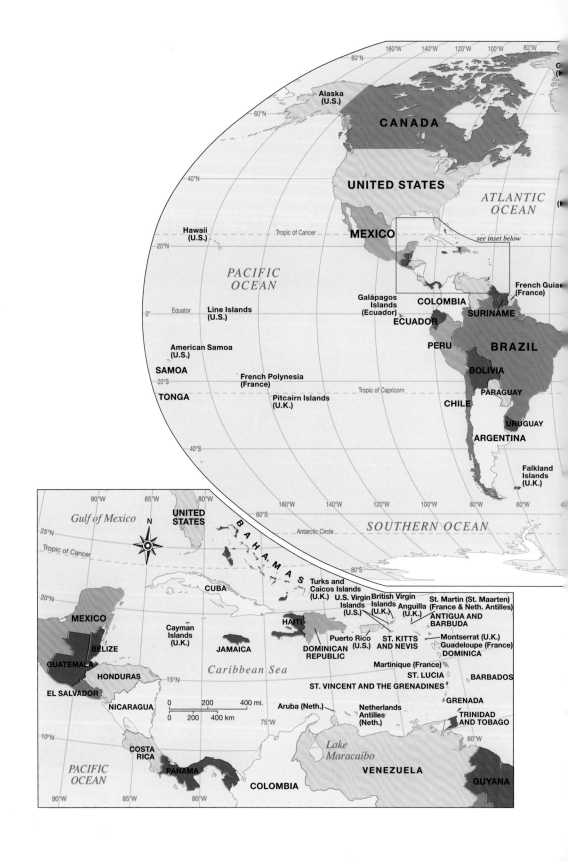

160°W   140°W   120°W   100°W   80°W

80°N

Alaska
(U.S.)

60°N

CANADA

40°N

UNITED STATES

*ATLANTIC
OCEAN*

Hawaii
(U.S.)   Tropic of Cancer

20°N   **MEXICO**   see inset below

*PACIFIC
OCEAN*

Galápagos   French Guiana
Islands   **COLOMBIA**   (France)
(Ecuador)

Equator   Line Islands   **SURINAME**
(U.S.)   **ECUADOR**

0°

American Samoa   **PERU**   **BRAZIL**
(U.S.)

SAMOA   **BOLIVIA**

French Polynesia
20°S   (France)   **PARAGUAY**

TONGA   Pitcairn Islands   Tropic of Capricorn
(U.K.)   **CHILE**

URUGUAY

ARGENTINA

40°S

Falkland
Islands
(U.K.)

160°W   140°W   120°W   100°W   80°W   60°W

60°S

SOUTHERN OCEAN

Antarctic Circle

80°S

90°W   85°W   80°W   **UNITED
STATES**

Gulf of Mexico   N

25°N   B
Tropic of Cancer   A
H
A
M
A
S

20°N   **CUBA**   Turks and
Caicos Islands   St. Martin (St. Maarten)
(U.K.) U.S. Virgin British Virgin (France & Neth. Antilles)
Islands Islands Anguilla **ANTIGUA AND**
(U.S.)   (U.K.)   (U.K.)   **BARBUDA**
MEXICO
Cayman   **HAITI**
Islands   Montserrat (U.K.)
(U.K.)   Puerto Rico **ST. KITTS** Guadeloupe (France)
BELIZE   **JAMAICA** (U.S.) **AND NEVIS** **DOMINICA**
**DOMINICAN
GUATEMALA**   **REPUBLIC**
Caribbean Sea   Martinique (France)
HONDURAS   **ST. LUCIA**   **BARBADOS**
15°N
EL SALVADOR   **ST. VINCENT AND THE GRENADINES**
0   200   400 mi.   **GRENADA**
NICARAGUA   Aruba (Neth.)   Netherlands
0   200   400 km   Antilles   **TRINIDAD
75°W   (Neth.)   AND TOBAGO**
10°N
**COSTA
RICA**   *Lake
Maracaibo*
*PACIFIC
OCEAN*   **PANAMA**   **VENEZUELA**   **GUYANA**
COLOMBIA
90°W   85°W   80°W   60°W

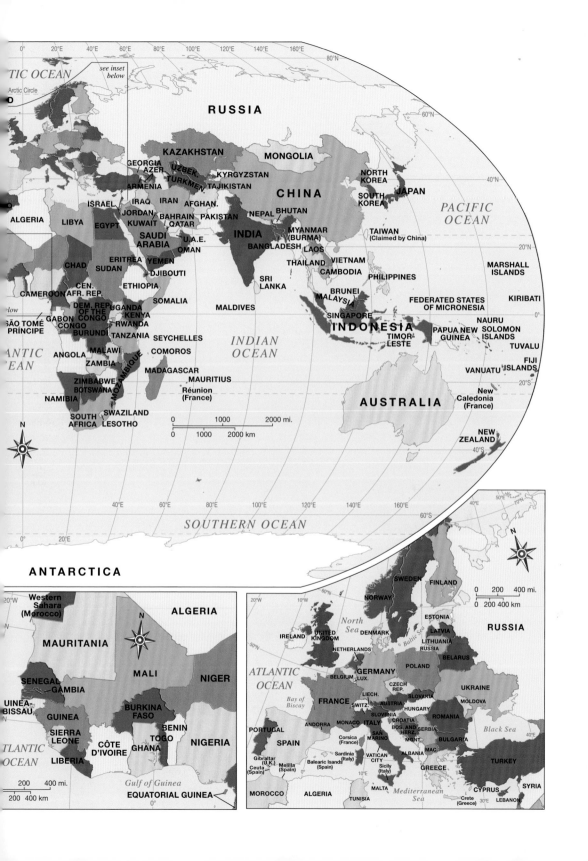

CHAPTER 1

Historical Background on the Cuban Missile Crisis

The Cuban Missile Crisis: An Overview

John Merriman and Jay Winter

The Cuban missile crisis took place in October 1962, brought on in great part by Soviet and U.S. hostility and anxieties that had been building for a long time. Cuba's revolutionary leader Fidel Castro feared that the United States was going to invade the island, contributing to the crisis. The event proved to be the closest the world had ever come to full-scale nuclear war. Acutely aware of how close they had come to a worldwide disaster, European and North American leaders determined not to risk the danger again. To help ensure this, they invoked changes that dramatically altered the system of international relations. John Merriman is the Charles Seymour Professor of History at Yale University. Jay Winter is the Charles J. Stille Professor of History at Yale University.

Photo on previous page: Fidel Castro led Cuba during the 1962 crisis involving Russian missiles placed on the island nation. (Lee Lockwood/ Time Life Pictures/Getty Images.)

SOURCE. *Europe Since 1914: Encyclopedia of the Age of War and Reconstruction.* Belmont, CA: Charles Scribner's Sons, 2006. Copyright © 2006 by Gale, Cengage Learning. Reproduced by permission of Gale, a part of Cengage Learning.

The Cuban Missile Crisis of October 1962 is the closest the world has ever come to full-scale nuclear war, and fear of the narrow means by which true disaster was averted frightened European and North American leaders into changes that dramatically altered the international system. . . .

The Roots of the Conflict

Cuba was the focus of the crisis, but the roots of this conflict lay in long-standing Soviet and U.S. antagonism and insecurities. The country had become a thorn in the side of U.S. leaders following Fidel Castro's seizure of power in 1959. Analysts in Washington debated Castro's faith in communism, but whatever his leanings, U.S. policy makers believed their reputation in Latin America could not tolerate a truly radical state only ninety miles from Florida. Castro's threats to nationalize foreign property on the island might seem a dangerous example to revolutionary groups throughout a region long considered a U.S. sphere of influence, they reasoned, while Cuba was simply too close for comfort for U.S. leaders ever vigilant against communist outposts. President Dwight D. Eisenhower endorsed Castro's overthrow as early as January 1960, a year before breaking diplomatic relations with his regime. By the time John F. Kennedy took office the following year vowing to "oppose aggression or subversion anywhere in the Americas," plans for a U.S.-supported invasion by Cuban exiles were already advanced, and the new president approved the operation with minimal oversight.

The failed Bay of Pigs invasion of April 1961 proved one of Kennedy's greatest fiascos. He publicly took full responsibility but swore thereafter to hold more tightly

> Soviet missiles in Cuba offered the Kremlin . . . the ability to destroy Washington without warning while decimating America's missile deterrent as well.

to the reins of power lest others drive his administration to ruin. He appointed his most trusted advisors, including his brother, Attorney General Robert F. Kennedy, to oversee Cuba policy, making Castro's removal one of his highest priorities. Cuba's affect on U.S. security and prestige, the president believed, threatened to tilt the Cold War's delicate balance in communism's favor.

The Cuban-Soviet Alliance

Correctly believing that U.S. leaders sought his fall from power, Castro sought Moscow's protection, a move the Soviets embraced. Premier Nikita Khrushchev in particular sought greater parity [balance] in U.S.-Soviet relations by the early 1960s and believed Washington's greater nuclear strength, including its nuclear missiles stationed along the Soviet border in Turkey, ensured that the Americans held the better hand in any superpower clash. The two communist leaders therefore decided in May 1962, for reasons both believed were defensive, to deploy to Cuba some eighty nuclear missiles, with range enough to place virtually the entire continental United States—including the newly constructed American missile fields in the Dakotas—within Moscow's sights. "Installation of our missiles in Cuba would, I thought, restrain the United States from precipitous military action against Castro's government," Khrushchev later recounted, and "equalized what the West likes to call the 'balance of power'." . . . Washington saw things differently. Soviet missiles in Cuba offered the Kremlin a true first-strike capability, including the ability to destroy Washington without warning while decimating America's missile deterrent as well. Surely the Kremlin would not risk this dangerous move, Kennedy's intelligence team incorrectly determined a full five months *after* Khrushchev ordered the missile deployment. If Cuba should "become an offensive military base of significant capacity for the Soviet Union," Kennedy publicly warned, "then this country will do whatever must be done to protect its own security and that of its allies."

The U.S. Blockade of Cuba

Kennedy was therefore infuriated to learn, on 16 October, that a U.S. spy plane had captured photos of Soviet missile-site construction in Cuba. His national security team hastily developed three options for removing the threat: invasion, negotiations, or blockade of the island. While his more hawkish advisors called for an immediate strike, on 22 October Kennedy announced a "quarantine" around Cuba. Soviet leaders vowed their ships would not respect the American blockade, and Khrushchev warned that Kennedy was pushing "mankind towards the abyss." Soviet ships eventually halted just short of the quarantine line two days later, but as missile-site construction continued in Cuba, each side continued to prepare for war.

> The ramifications of this near brush with disaster dramatically changed the course of the Cold War.

Cooler heads eventually prevailed. Public blustering continued, but private discussions . . . eventually developed a usable compromise. The Soviets would remove the missiles following a U.S. pledge not to invade Cuba, while Kennedy promised to remove his missiles from Turkey (after a politically prudent six-month interval). . . . By 28 October full-scale war had been averted. . . . Only Castro seemed displeased by the peaceful conclusion of the crisis. Having been ready to sacrifice his country's existence for the sake of its independence, indeed having urged Khrushchev to strike the United States, Castro felt betrayed by what he termed the Kremlin's "surprising, sudden, and unconditional surrender." It would take several years and millions in aid before he would trust the Soviets again.

U.S. and Soviet Reaction to the Crisis

The ramifications of this near brush with disaster dramatically changed the course of the Cold War, and Europe's role in the conflict especially. Kennedy proved shaken by the nearness of the conflict and resolved thereafter to limit the risk of nuclear warfare. He authorized a direct "hot line" between the White House and the Kremlin so that leaders could communicate directly during any future crisis, and a U.S.-led ban on atmospheric nuclear tests followed. . . .

Soviet leaders drew similar and different conclusions from the conflict, shaped by their perception that they had lost the confrontation because of the very disparity of power that the missile deployment in Cuba had been designed to eliminate in the first place. On the one hand, Khrushchev left the conflict as shaken as Kennedy. What was needed was a "relaxation of tension," he told his U.S. counterpart. Others within his government preached strength, however. "You Americans will never be able to do this to us again," one Soviet diplomat warned, and while U.S. leaders focused on countering communist insurgents throughout the developing world, Soviet policy makers thereafter focused primarily on narrowing the nuclear gap. . . .

Other Reactions to the Crisis

The Cuban Missile Crisis altered European and Asian diplomacy as well. Chinese leaders forged ahead with their own nascent nuclear program in its wake, determined never again to let Moscow take the lead in the East-West conflict. Relaxation of U.S.-Soviet tensions . . . proved that both countries only sought "domination of the world by the two great despots," China's foreign minister charged. . . .

France's Charles de Gaulle would not have put the idea any differently. The Cuban crisis reinforced his long-standing view that French power was needed as a coun-

Bay of Pigs

The small island-nation [of Cuba] had been a source of great pain to Americans ever since the bearded, baseball-loving Fidel Castro Ruz emerged from his hideout in the mountains of the Sierra Maestra, marched six hundred miles over seven days down Cuba's Central Highway, arrived in Havana to seize the reins of power left vacant by the fleeing dictator Fulgencio Batista, and then declared himself a communist and enemy to the United States.

In the spring of 1961 [U.S. president John F.] Kennedy approved a CIA plan that had a group of Cuban émigrés . . . storm the coast of Cuba at the swamp-filled Bay of Pigs, 150 miles south of Havana. They would then run to the mountains, inspire a revolt of anti-Castro movements already on the island, and call on the United States for support. But, aware in advance of the plan (word of an American-backed coup had been circulating for months throughout Central America), Castro's modest air force simply met the émigrés and quickly cleared the beach of them.

The invasion was more than a failure; it was a fiasco. It had been too lim-

terweight to Soviet and U.S. balancing, and he was particularly incensed when Kennedy chose to only "inform" him of events during the crisis rather than "consult." . . . Cuba proved to de Gaulle that an independently strong France was needed for a true balance of powers, even if limits on French international cooperation followed.

British leaders had already reached a similar conclusion on the need for an alternative to bipolarity and on the central importance of nuclear weapons to true great power status because, as Prime Minister Harold Macmillan quipped, "We must rely on the power of the nuclear deterrent, or we must throw up the sponge!" . . . Macmillan's government was particularly infuriated with Washington's public expectation of unwavering support during the Cuban crisis, but unlike de Gaulle, British analysts determined to work to reform superpower rela-

ited to succeed, and yet those very limits were essential if the United States were to maintain the myth that the invasion was an indigenous uprising, springing from the hearts and minds of anti-Castro Cubans. Kennedy took four days to admit to the American people what much of the rest of the world already knew: that the Bay of Pigs was an American operation, conducted in secrecy without even the benefit of congressional sanction. And by then, much damage had been done to the American image, both at home and abroad.

Had there been no Bay of Pigs invasion, or had the invasion been a success instead of a humiliation, had it been the first sign of President Kennedy's skills at international affairs instead of a dangerous display of incompetence, the world may never have faced the terrible events that were to follow, events that would bring humanity to the edge of Armageddon and serve as the defining moment of the Cold War.

SOURCE: *Peter Jennings and Todd Brewster,* The Century. *New York: Doubleday, 1998, p. 373.*

tions from within rather than to break outright with the Americans. . . .

The German Reaction to the Crisis

Not every state chose nuclear parity as the answer to the East-West divide. German leaders . . . feared in particular their geographic peril. Set between the warring superpowers, indeed divided by them, German leaders pushed hardest for détente [easing of tensions] following 1962, because as Chancellor Konrad Adenauer explained even before the Cuban stalemate, any future war in Europe "would be a nuclear war . . . without any profit for the survivors." His was a common sentiment throughout the Continent, and with a wall bisecting the ancient

'There is no hope for us . . . if there is no change.'

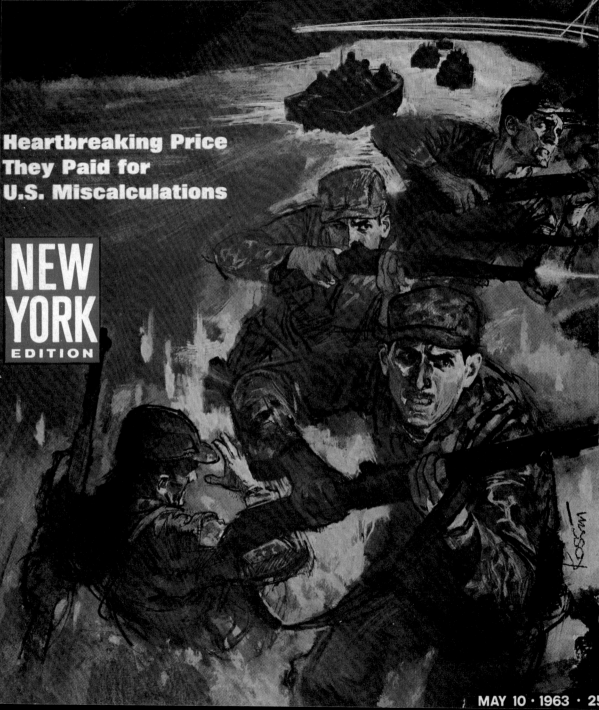

LIFE

RAW UNTOLD TRUTH
BY MEN WHO FOUGHT
Bay of Pigs

Heartbreaking Price
They Paid for
U.S. Miscalculations

NEW YORK EDITION

MAY 10 · 1963 · 25

capital of Berlin since 1961, German leaders led the charge following the Cuban Missile Crisis toward East-West reconciliation. . . . "There is no hope for us," West Berlin Mayor Willy Brandt concluded after the Cuban Missile Crisis, "if there is no change." . . .

Castro left the crisis the only real winner, while superpower bipolarity endured its death-blow. The tense October days allowed the Cuban leader to solidify his tenuous hold on power, and for the remaining decades of the Cold War he remained a favorite ally in Moscow and notorious in Washington. Neither Kennedy nor Khrushchev survived in power long after the affair, and their departure symbolized the way the Cuban Missile Crisis, in many ways the low point of the Cold War brought on by the logic of a world divided in two, revealed to observers throughout the world, and to Europeans especially, the need to find a third way.

Image on previous page: Many observers see the roots of the Cuban missile crisis in the failed 1961 U.S. invasion of Cuba, known to Americans as the Bay of Pigs, an incident illustrated on this magazine cover from the era. (Sanford Kossin/Time & Life Pictures/Getty Images.)

Reconnaissance Photos Chart the Birth of a Crisis

Relman Morin

The following viewpoint from the November 5, 1962, edition of the American newspaper the *Daily Telegram* focuses on U.S. photo reconnaissance missions over Cuba and the role they played in the Cuban missile crisis. The film from the missions provided the United States with evidence of the Soviet military buildup in Cuba. The photos were carefully analyzed and used to chart the Soviet nuclear threat to the United States as it took shape on Cuban bases. U.S. president John F. Kennedy used the photographs and slides of the Soviet rocket installations in Cuba to justify to the Soviets and the rest of the world a blockade of Cuba. Relman Morin was a journalist, war correspondent, Pulitzer Prize winner, and author of a number of books, including *Assassination: The Death of President John F. Kennedy*.

SOURCE. Relman Morin, "Process of Putting Together Evidence from Cuba 'Slow,'" *Daily Telegram*, vol. LXVII, no. 263, November 5, 1962, p. 1.

Imagine a strip of photographic film, 20 to 30 feet wide, some six miles long. Cut in sections, it is stretched across the floor. Photo analysts, on hands and knees, crawl around on the pictures, peering at them through steromicroscopes, special magnifying glasses. The technicians note any detail of change in terrain. More especially, they look for objects on the sites that weren't there yesterday.

They chartered the birth of a crisis, a Soviet nuclear threat to the U.S. swiftly taking shape on Cuban bases.

Missions Result in U.S. Quarantine

Beginning Monday, Oct. 15 [1962], says a chief of intelligence, American pilots flew six and seven photo reconnaissance missions over Cuba daily.

"We blanketed the island," he says.

The planes brought back miles of film.

Today, you look at a sequence of pictures taken above a missile site. The first shots show empty country. Then, apparently out of thin air, construction becomes visible in succeeding days—an anti-aircraft, a half-completed security fence, prefabricated concrete arches, a plant for making cement, launching pads, fire control bunkers, an earth-molded structure, revetments [barricades].

It was this evidence that impelled [U.S.] President [John F.] Kennedy to declare a quarantine on shipments of offensive weapons to Cuba, and to demand the dismantling of the missile sites already built.

Republicans have attacked Kennedy on the ground that he acted too slowly.

Sen. [Hugh] Scott (R-Pa) says "very hard information" about the Soviet sites was available in mid-September. Sen. [Kenneth] Keating (R-NY), in a similar assertion, said Sept. 8 that a blockade of Cuba might be necessary.

But a top intelligence agent gives this version:

Late August—Cuban refugees report the arrival of Soviet technicians in Cuba and the erection of rocket launchers. The refugees are carefully interrogated. Checks on the sites show they are surface-to-air launchers, and "cruise sites," coastal missile artillery. Their range is too short to reach the U.S.

> "The missiles and the bombers are offensive weapons."

Mid-September—A U2 plane belonging to the Chinese Nationalists on Formosa is shot down over Communist China. U2 flights over Cuba are suspended "until we could learn what brought down the plane in China."

Did the Russians have some new gadget, capable of reaching and destroying a U2, flying above 70,000 feet? "If so," the officer says, "there was the possibility that we wouldn't be able to get any more high-altitude photos—which are better because they show more—out of Cuba." Low-flying planes, often coming in at altitudes of 300 to 800 feet, continue the surveillance. The officer won't disclose what brought down the U2 in China.

Photos Reveal Soviet Activities and Missiles

Late September—"We began to be uneasy because of the large numbers of Russian ships coming to Cuba. They never carried missiles on deck, always in the holds. This became apparent later."

Sept. 28—Photo of a Soviet freighter shows some large crates on deck. In the picture, they look cylindrical, like miniature Quonset huts. Evaluation indicates they are probably Ilyushin-28s [IL-28s], a Soviet light bomber with a range of 750 miles. These crates are unloaded in remote ports, not Havana, and solely by the Russians, not the Cubans.

Late Sept. to Oct. 1—Cuban refugees report heavy nighttime truck traffic on the highways. The freight is covered. It appears to be larger than ordinary cargo.

Early October—Bad weather and clouds over Cuba cause a second suspension of the reconnaissance flights.

Oct. 14—A photo mission reveals sites under construction. They are for medium rockets, range 1,000 miles, and for intermediates, range 2,000 miles. On the same day, pictures are taken of the cylindrical crates, seen Sept. 28 on the freighter, now at San Juliano airport. Now it is confirmed that the assembly for the IL-28s was in the crates. The missiles and the bombers are offensive weapons.

Oct. 15—These photographs are evaluated in the early evening. They touch off the [chain] of events that led to the quarantine.

Pictures taken from U.S. spy planes over Cuba revealed the presence of Russian missile installations on the Caribbean island nation. (**Hulton Archive/Getty Images.**)

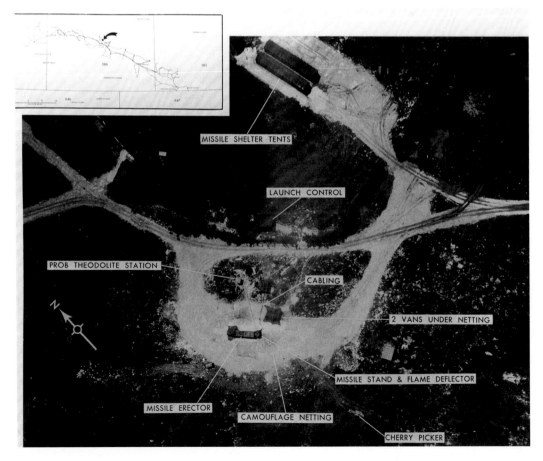

MISSILE SHELTER TENTS

LAUNCH CONTROL

PROB THEODOLITE STATION

CABLING

2 VANS UNDER NETTING

MISSILE STAND & FLAME DEFLECTOR

MISSILE ERECTOR

CAMOUFLAGE NETTING

CHERRY PICKER

MISSILE SITES AND BASES IN CUBA, 1962

Medium-range nuclear missile sites

Intermediate-range nuclear missile sites

S SAM sites

M Missile bases

C Coastal defense conventional cruise missile sites

Motorized rifle regiments

Airfields

Ports

Taken from: Michael Dobbs, *One Minute to Midnight*. New York: Knopf, 2008. pp. x–xi.

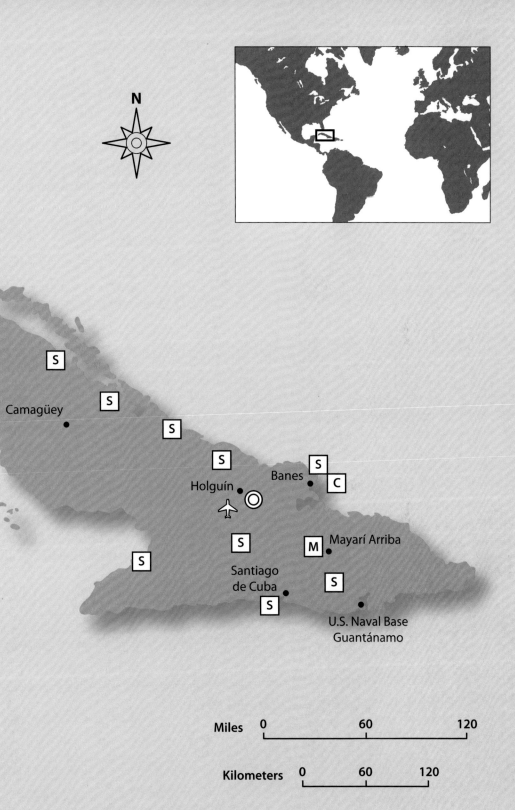

N

Camagüey

Holguín ✈ ◎

Banes

Mayarí Arriba

Santiago
de Cuba

U.S. Naval Base
Guantánamo

Miles   0   60   120

Kilometers   0   60   120

"I think, but I can't prove absolutely, that the Russians started the construction work about Oct. 10 to 22," the intelligence agent says.

By Oct. 19, at San Diego Los Banos, photographs showed seven missiles, four erectors, 100 vehicles, and tents for 500 men. The base became operational in three days, the officer said.

The United States Reacts

"The problem was to confirm the available evidence, assess the magnitude, and determine the nature of the Soviet threat," he says. He and members of his staff worked 34 hours without sleep to accomplish this, he said.

The Soviet objective was described as "a rapid secret simultaneous deployment" of the missile bases.

"In this day and age," the officer observed, "even the rapid development of a weapons site is a casus belli" (provocation to war).

Before the end of the week of Oct. 15, the evidence was clear. The President was preparing to present it in his statement ordering the quarantine. Kennedy was ready to make it on Sunday, Oct. 21, but Secretary of State [Dean] Rusk persuaded him to wait a day, saying it would be difficult to pre-notify all the ambassadors on a weekend.

On Monday, Oct. 22, an hour before the President spoke, representatives of the NATO [North Atlantic Treaty Organization], SEATO [Southeast Asia Treaty Organization], and CENTO [Central Treaty Organization] alliances were invited to the State Department. Waiting for them was Roger Hilsman, director of the Bureau of Intelligence and Research.

He presented the American findings, showing photographs and slides of the Soviet rocket installations in Cuba. Later, he delivered the same briefing to representatives of the neutral nations.

The general impression is that the U.S. case was wholly persuasive.

At 6 P.M., Soviet Ambassador Anatoly F. Dobrynin was called to Rusk's office. He emerged 85 minutes later. Rusk had told him about the blockade of Cuba. The ambassador, normally a bluff cheerful-looking man, seemed shaken.

Says an agent, "We caught them with their launchers down and their rockets showing."

U.S. President Kennedy Orders a Blockade of Cuba

Edward T. Folliard

The following viewpoint from the October 23, 1962, edition of the *Washington Post* documents the speech given by U.S. president John F. Kennedy regarding the military buildup in Cuba. He announces that in response to the buildup, the United States has ordered a blockade of Cuba to turn back ships hauling offensive weapons. He warns that the United States will not tolerate continued offensive military buildup in Cuba and states that he has directed the U.S. military to prepare for any possible occurrence. He accuses the Soviet Union of deliberate deception and appeals to the Soviet premier to end the arms race. Edward T. Folliard was a Pulitzer Prize–winning journalist who served as White House correspondent for the *Washington Post* from 1923 to 1967.

President Kennedy told the Nation—and world—last night, that the Russians had built offensive nuclear missile bases in Cuba, and announced that the United States has ordered a blockade of the Communist-ruled island to turn back ships hauling offensive weapons.

> 'The purpose of these bases . . . can be none other than to provide a nuclear strike capability against the Western Hemisphere.'

He said that if the offensive military buildup in Cuba continues, thus increasing the threat to the Western Hemisphere, further action will come.

"I have directed the armed forces to prepare for any eventualities," he said. Mr. Kennedy said he had "hard information" that the Cuban bases were equipped to fire medium-range missiles with nuclear warheads more than 1000 miles, a range that would take in Washington and Mexico City.

He said bases under construction but not yet completed, appear to be designed for intermediate-range ballistic missiles that travel as far as Hudson Bay, Canada, and as far south as Lima, Peru. Their range is considered to be about 2200 miles.

"The purpose of these bases," the President emphasized, "can be none other than to provide a nuclear strike capability against the Western Hemisphere."

"It shall be the policy of this Nation," Mr. Kennedy said, "to regard any nuclear missile launching from Cuba against any nation in the Western Hemisphere as an attack by the Soviet Union on the United States requiring a full retaliatory response upon the Soviet Union."

The Chief Executive in effect accused the Soviet Government and Soviet Foreign Minister Andrei

> "I call upon Chairman Khrushchev . . . to halt and eliminate this clandestine, reckless and provocative threat to world peace and to stable relations between our two nations."

Gromyko of lying in saying that the Russian arms being sent to Cuba were purely for defensive purposes.

Besides ordering the blockade Mr. Kennedy ordered a reinforcement of the United States Navy base at Guantanamo, Cuba, and announced the evacuation yesterday of the dependents of fighting personnel at the base.

He said he was asking for an emergency meeting "without delay" of the United Nations Security Council to "take action against this latest Soviet threat to world peace." He added he was also calling for a meeting of the Organ of Consultation under the Organization of American States to consider the threat to hemispheric security.

Appeals to Khrushchev

"I call upon Chairman Khrushchev," he said, "to halt and eliminate this clandestine, reckless and provocative threat to world peace and to stable relations between our two nations."

The President not only told the Soviet Premier that the United States would retaliate against the Soviet Union with a nuclear assault if missiles were launched from Cuba against any nation in the Western Hemisphere, but said:

"Any hostile move anywhere in the world against the safety and freedom of peoples to whom we are committed—including in particular the brave people of West Berlin—will be met by whatever action is needed."

Speaks 19 Minutes

Mr. Kennedy had been allotted a half hour by the television and radio networks, but he used up only 19 minutes as he faced the cameras and microphones in his office in the West Wing.

"Let no one doubt that this is a difficult and dangerous effort on which we have set out," he said toward the end. "No one can foresee precisely what course it will take or what costs or casualties will be incurred.

"Many months of sacrifice and self-discipline lie ahead—months in which both our will and our patience will be tested. . . . But the greatest danger of all would be to do nothing."

He said America's goal was not the victory of might but the vindication of right—peace and freedom around the world.

"God willing," he said, "that goal will be achieved."

Urges A-Race End

He called on the Soviet Premier further to "abandon this course of world domination, and to join in an historic

Many Americans learned about the 1962 blockade of Cuba when president John F. Kennedy announced it on television. (Ralph Crane/Time & Life Pictures/Getty Images.)

effort to end the perilous arms race and transform the history of man."

"He has an opportunity now," he said of Khrushchev, "to move the world back from the abyss of destruction, by returning to his Government's own words that it had no need to station missiles outside its own territory, and withdrawing these weapons from Cuba, by refraining from any action which will widen or deepen the present crisis, and then by participating in a search for peaceful and permanent solutions."

> 'Neither the United States nor the world community of nations can tolerate deliberate deception and offensive threats on the part of any nation, large or small.'

After accusing the Soviet Government of making a "false" statement in saying that the arms it was sending Cuba were for purely defensive purposes, the President said:

"Only last Thursday as evidence of this rapid buildup was already in my hand, Soviet Foreign Minister Gromyko told me in my office that he was instructed to make it clear once again, as he said his Government already had done, that Soviet assistance to Cuba 'pursued solely the purpose of contributing to the defense capabilities of Cuba,' that 'training by Soviet specialists of Cuban nationalists in handling defensive armaments was by no means offensive,' and that if it were otherwise, the Soviet Government would never become involved in rendering such assistance.

"That statement also was false."

"Deliberate Deception"

The President went on to say that "neither the United States nor the world community of nations can tolerate deliberate deception and offensive threats on the part of any nation, large or small."

"We no longer live in a world where only the actual firing of weapons represents a sufficient challenge to a nation's security to constitute a maximum peril," he said. "Nuclear weapons are so destructive, and ballistic missiles are so swift, that any substantially increased possibility of their use or any sudden change in their

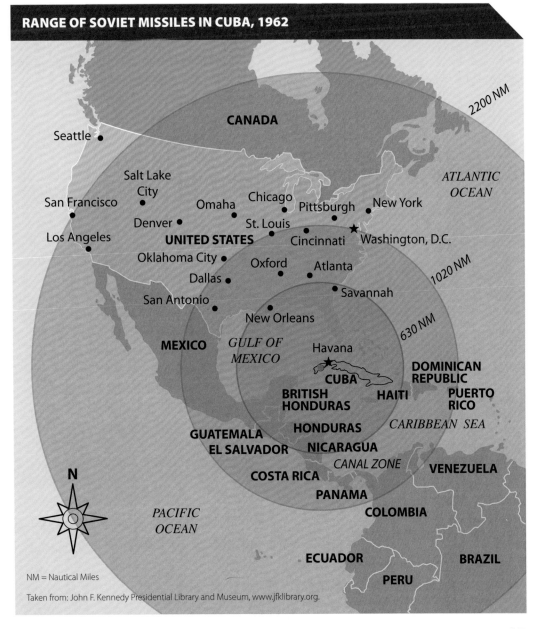

RANGE OF SOVIET MISSILES IN CUBA, 1962

2200 NM

CANADA

Seattle

Salt Lake City

ATLANTIC OCEAN

San Francisco

Omaha

Chicago

Pittsburgh

New York

Denver

St. Louis

Los Angeles

UNITED STATES

Cincinnati

Washington, D.C.

Oklahoma City

Oxford

Atlanta

1020 NM

Dallas

San Antonio

Savannah

New Orleans

630 NM

MEXICO

GULF OF MEXICO

Havana

DOMINICAN REPUBLIC

CUBA

BRITISH HONDURAS

HAITI

PUERTO RICO

GUATEMALA

HONDURAS

CARIBBEAN SEA

EL SALVADOR

NICARAGUA

CANAL ZONE

VENEZUELA

N

COSTA RICA

PANAMA

COLOMBIA

PACIFIC OCEAN

ECUADOR

BRAZIL

PERU

NM = Nautical Miles

Taken from: John F. Kennedy Presidential Library and Museum, www.jfklibrary.org.

deployment may well be regarded as a definite threat to the peace."

The Chief Executive said the actions he already has ordered might "only be the beginning."

"We will not prematurely or unnecessarily risk the costs of world-wide nuclear war in which even the fruits of victory would be ashes in our mouth," he said, "but neither will we shrink from that risk at any time it must faced."

He then went on to say that, under the authority entrusted to him by the Constitution as endorsed by a recent resolution of Congress, he was taking these "initial" steps immediately:

1. Action to halt the offensive buildup in Cuba, by ordering a quarantine on all offensive military equipment under shipment to that island. All ships of any kind, from whatever nation or port, found to contain cargoes of offensive weapons, will be turned back. The quarantine, if necessary, will be extended to other types of cargoes and carriers—but the necessities of life will not be barred from Cuba.

2. Continued and increased close surveillance of Cuba and its military buildup. If the buildup continues, further action will be justified—and he has directed the armed forces "to prepare for any eventualities."

3. Readiness to retaliate against the Soviet Union in the event of any missile attack from Cuba on any nation in the Western Hemisphere, an act which the United States will regard as a Soviet attack.

4. As a necessary military precaution reinforcement of the U.S. base at Guantanamo in Cuba, with additional military units put on an alert basis, and dependents evacuated.

5. A call for an immediate meeting of the Organ of Consultation under the Organization of American

States. The meeting will consider the threat to hemi-spheric security and the invoking of Articles 6 and 8 of the Rio Treaty to support all necessary action. The United Nations Charter allows for regional security arrangements—and "the nations of this Hemisphere decided long ago against the military presence of outside powers." America's other allies around the world also have been alerted.

6. A request, under the Charter of the United Nations, for an emergency meeting of the Security Council to take action against "this latest Soviet threat to world peace."

7. An appeal to Premier Khrushchev to "halt and elimi-nate this clandestine, reckless and provocative threat to world peace."

The UN Security Council Debates the Cuban Crisis

The *Times'* United Nations correspondent

In the following viewpoint, the United Nations correspondent for the British newspaper the *Times* reports on the October 1962 United Nations Security Council meetings on the Cuban crisis. During the debate, Britain supported the United States's stance, arguing that the Soviet missiles in Cuba had been installed "in secrecy" and "behind a mask of duplicity" and must be dismantled and removed. Meanwhile, forty-three other member nations of the United Nations—who remained uncommitted to the conflicting American and Soviet draft resolutions regarding the actions to be taken—worked behind the scenes to come up with a third option. At the same time, Latin American countries agreed that this latest move in Cuba signified a genuine threat to their security.

SOURCE. "Britain Urges Removal of Missiles," *Times*, October 25, 1962, p. 8. Copyright © 1962 Times Newspapers Ltd. Reproduced by permission.

Britain placed herself firmly alongside the United States when the [United Nations] Security Council debate on the Cuban crisis began today. [Britain's UN representative] Sir Patrick Dean told its members: "The only way now to restore confidence in the western hemisphere is for these offensive missiles [in Cuba] to be dismantled and withdrawn. Only then can we believe the honesty of the pronouncements by the Soviet and Cuban leaders that they have no aggressive intentions."

The Search for a Compromise

While the council continued to discuss the crisis in a grim mood, behind the scenes a group of some 43 uncommitted countries were seeking actively to promote a compromise. These representatives held a long meeting last night, and today a committee of seven, headed by Mr. Rossides, of Cyprus (acting as chairman of the

The UN security council chamber, seen here standing empty, was the site of fierce debates over Cuba's missiles. (**Spencer Platt/Getty Images.**)

group), conferred privately for nearly an hour with U Thant, the acting Secretary-General.

The group, not all of whose members are necessarily opposed to the American action, though they are fearful of its consequences, is understood to be aiming at a third course of action as against those proposed in the conflicting American and Russian draft resolutions. This may involve asking U Thant to appeal to the United States, the Soviet Union, and Cuba to take no action which would exacerbate the situation.

The Drafting of a Motion

At last night's meeting some confirmed "neutralists" argued that the only solution was to call for a return to the status quo on October 22 [1962]. This would, in effect, mean that the United States would be asked to call off its blockade, while Cuba would be left with the missile bases it now has and Russia would now undertake not to reinforce them. However, this proposal was not adopted by the group as a whole.

Indications are that when the Security Council meets again tonight, Ghana and the United Arab Republic (the two Afro-Asian members of the Security Council) may co-sponsor a resolution, asking U Thant to use his good offices in the dispute.

> 'By no stretch even of the Soviet imagination can a nuclear missile with a range of over 2,000 miles in Cuba be called defensive.'

The exact form of the motion has not yet been decided; it is still being drafted by a committee consisting of Cyprus, Ghana, the United Arab Republic, Algeria, Iraq, Sierra Leone, and Yugoslavia.

Not all the 53 countries present at last night's meeting are expected to support this resolution. For instance, it is learnt that certain countries like Sweden attended the meeting only as observers, and they have decided to take no further part in the group's activities.

The Effort to Reach a Decision

Whether or not much comes of this mediatory move, the fact that today is the seventeenth anniversary of United Nations Day seems to have had a mollifying influence on the atmosphere at this headquarters. The celebrations were highlighted by a concert this afternoon given by the Leningrad Philharmonic Orchestra and the violinist Mr. David Oistrakh, and this caused the General Assembly and the committees, as well as the Security Council, to suspend their activities for the nonce [present occasion].

The council, however, was continuing its meeting this evening, and it may remain in session until far into the night in an effort to reach a decision. So far six member states have spoken. Of these, four—Britain, Venezuela, Ireland, and the United States—have supported the American blockade of Cuba. Russia and Rumania have condemned it and so has Cuba, which, however, is not a member of the council and does not have the right to vote.

The British View

In a speech this morning, Sir Patrick Dean said that neither Mr. [Valerian] Zorin [ambassador] of Russia nor Dr. [Mario] Garcia-Inchaustegui [ambassador] of Cuba had yesterday denied before the council that the Soviet Union had furnished missiles to Cuba, and "by no stretch even of the Soviet imagination can a nuclear missile with a range of over 2,000 miles in Cuba be called defensive."

Sir Patrick added that these weapons of mass destruction were being installed in secrecy and "behind a mask of duplicity." Such calculated double dealing was bound to throw a sinister light on the intentions of the Soviet Government.

The only motive for embarking on such a dangerous course, said Sir Patrick, could be that the Soviet Union hoped to increase the area of communist domination and gain a significant military advantage in favour of the communist block. The truth of the matter, he said, was that the threat today came not from without against Cuba, but from within Cuba against its neighbours.

A Threat to World Security

It was the consensus of the Latin American countries that this latest move in Cuba represented a real threat to their security, went on Sir Patrick. Britain agreed with their assessment. "Furthermore, if they are threatened then we are threatened too. For in this nuclear age the whole free world stands or falls together."

The U.S. Offers the Soviet Union an Opportunity to Negotiate

Laurence Burd

The following viewpoint from the October 28, 1962, *Chicago Daily Tribune* focuses on the letters exchanged between U.S. president John F. Kennedy and Soviet premier Nikita Khrushchev regarding the Cuban crisis. Khrushchev offers to dismantle the Cuban bases if the United States agrees to do away with its intermediate-range missile bases in Turkey. Kennedy offers to negotiate with Russia, but not until all work is stopped on missile sites and the Cuban bases are dismantled and removed. Kennedy assures Khrushchev that as soon as the Cuban bases are scrapped, the United States will lift its naval quarantine of Cuba and "give assurances against an invasion of Cuba." Laurence Burd served first as a Washington correspondent for the *Chicago Tribune* and the *Los Angeles Times* and then as a

---

SOURCE. Laurence Burd, "Kennedy Offers to Negotiate If Reds Abandon Missile Sites," *Chicago Daily Tribune*, October 28, 1962, pp. 1–2.

computer analyst for the Federal Reserve Board of the United States.

President [John F.] Kennedy tonight [October 27, 1962] offered to negotiate with Russia a "permanent solution to the Cuban problem" provided Russia agrees promptly to remove its missile bases from Cuba under effective United Nations supervision.

In a letter replying to a note yesterday from Premier Nikita Khrushchev of Russia, the President said that once the Cuban bases are scrapped the United States will remove its naval quarantine and "give assurances against an invasion of Cuba."

The President told Khrushchev that such a settlement on Cuba would ease world tensions and "enable us to work toward a more general arrangement regarding other armaments," as Khrushchev had mentioned.

The Kennedy letter replies specifically to the first of two Khrushchev letters received in the last 24 hours but also referred to the second Khrushchev letter in that period.

In his second letter, Khrushchev proposed a swap whereby Russia would dismantle the Cuban bases if the United States would scrap its intermediate range missile bases in Turkey, a North Atlantic Treaty Organization ally on Russia's borders.

The President's letter did not mention the Turkey-Cuba swap specifically, but said as the White House had earlier, that no fruitful negotiations to ease the crisis can be undertaken until the Cuban bases are dismantled.

"I would like to say again," Kennedy told Khrushchev, "that the United States is very much interested in reducing tensions and halting the

'The first ingredient is the cessation of work on missile sites in Cuba and measures to render such weapons inoperable, under effective international guarantees.'

arms race: and if your letter signifies that you are prepared to discuss a detente [easing of tensions] affecting
NATO and the Warsaw Pact, we are quite prepared to
consider with our allies any useful proposal.

"But the first ingredient is the cessation of work on
missile sites in Cuba and measures to render such weapons
inoperable, under effective international guarantees."

Kennedy told Khrushchev that the continued threat
posed by missiles in Cuba or prolonged discussions on
Cuba linking it to broad questions of European and world
security "would surely lead to an intensification of the
Cuban crisis and a grave risk to the peace of the world."

The Desire for a Prompt Solution

Although at the time the Kennedy letter was released the
Khrushchev note of yesterday had not been made public,
Kennedy's reply made it clear that Khrushchev in that
letter had not proposed a Cuba-Turkey bargain.

The President began his reply to Khrushchev by saying he welcomed the Russian premier's "statement of
your desire to seek a prompt solution to the problem."

The President told Khrushchev that assuming the
Russian bases in Cuba are promptly rendered inoperable,
the United States representatives at the United Nations
have been instructed to seek to work out this week-end
arrangements for a permanent solution along the lines
that Khrushchev's first letter proposed.

Kennedy said our representatives would cooperate
toward this end with acting United Nations Secretary
General U Thant, who is trying to mediate the dispute, and Russian representatives. In closing his letter,
Kennedy told Khrushchev, "I hope we can quickly agree
along the lines outlined in this letter and in your letter of
Oct. 26."

Announcement of the Kennedy letter was made
shortly after 8 P.M. by Pierre Salinger, White House press
secretary. His reply to the Khrushchev letter of last night

Nuclear diplomacy between President John F. Kennedy and Soviet premier Nikita Khrushchev (in easel photo, far right) in 1962 made possible the 2002 meeting of their children Caroline Kennedy (left) and Sergei Khrushchev. (**AP Images.**)

was much milder in tone than the response to the second Khrushchev letter made public to the world by radio Moscow in a broadcast this morning.

It was in this broadcast that Khrushchev offered to trade his bases in Cuba for the NATO sites in Turkey. Kennedy replied to this proposal in a White House statement within two hours by saying that no sensible negotiation could take place until the missile sites had been made inoperable and the shipment of further offensive weapons to Cuba be stopped.

No explanation was given by the White House why it had made public its answer to the second letter first this morning and then make public its reply to the first letter tonight. However, most observers pointed out that both Kennedy and Khrushchev were maintaining a cordial tone in the exchange of messages, if not in content.

A Statement from the White House

Kennedy appeared to be keeping the door open for negotiations in his letter while insisting that the Cuban missile cancer must first be removed.

Following is the text of the answer of President Kennedy made public in a statement from the White House:

"Several inconsistent and conflicting proposals have been made by the U.S.S.R. within the last 24 hours, including the one just made public [by radio] in Moscow. The proposal broadcast this morning involves the security of nations outside the western hemisphere countries and they alone that are subject to the threat that has produced the current crisis—the action of the Soviet government in secretly introducing offensive weapons into Cuba.

"Work on these offensive weapons is still proceeding at a rapid pace. The first imperative must be to deal with this immediate threat, under which no sensible negotiation can proceed.

"It is therefore the position of the United States that as an urgent preliminary to consideration of any proposals work on the Cuban bases must stop; offensive weapons must be rendered inoperable; and further shipment of offensive weapons to Cuba must cease—all under effective international verification.

"As to proposals concerning the security of nations outside this hemisphere, the United States and its allies have long taken the lead in seeking properly inspected arms limitation on both sides. These efforts can continue as soon as the present Soviet-created threat is ended."

Earlier this week, the defense department disclosed that the Russians have eight to 10 missile bases under construction on the Castro controlled island with each

> At least 5,000 Russians are reported to be in Cuba working on the bases.

base having "four launchers, more or less." The United States has released aerial photos of both medium and intermediate range missile sites. The photo of the intermediate base identifies a "probable nuclear warhead storage bunker."

Soviet and U.S. Missile Strength

At least 5,000 Russians are reported to be in Cuba working on the bases. More than 20 Russian IL-28 jet light bombers also are reported by the defense department to have arrived on the island.

The Red intermediate missiles are reported to have a range of at least 2,500 miles or enough to hit any major city in the United States with the possible exception of Seattle, Wash., if fired from Cuba.

The Jupiter intermediate range missile the United States has in Turkey near the Russian border has a range of at least 1,850 miles. It is a liquid propelled surface-to-surface missile with a nuclear warhead.

Although the defense department is silent on the Jupiter strength in Turkey, the United States is understood to have approximately 30 of the missiles in Turkey. The Jupiter also is in Italy. When the defense department announced two years ago that the Jupiter would be deployed in Italy and Turkey it was understood that each country would get two squadrons of 15 missiles each.

The Czech Media's Take on the Cuban Missile Crisis

Stanislav Koutnik

The following viewpoint from the December 26, 1962, *Christian Science Monitor* tells how the Czech media presented the Cuban missile crisis. It reports that all news in Czechoslovakia had to be politically correct—in line with the Communist view— so anything said against the Soviets was unacceptable slander and lies. Accordingly, the Czech media initially reported that there were no Soviet military installations in Cuba, nor were any being built. Furthermore, what U.S. president John F. Kennedy told the American people about the Soviet involvement in Cuba and its consequences was exaggerated and no more than propaganda designed to put economic, political, and psychological pressure on the Soviet Union. Stanislav Koutnik was a Czech journalist who wrote a number of articles for the *Christian Science Monitor*.

SOURCE. Stanislav Koutnik, "Cuba—As the Czechs Heard It," *Christian Science Monitor*, December 26, 1962, p. 16. Reproduced by permission of the author.

By the second day after President [John F.] Kennedy's historic announcement of the Cuban crisis, Radio Prague was comparing Mr. Kennedy with "Corporal Hitler." During the succeeding days, long after the Czechoslovaks had heard on overseas radio stations that America accused the Soviet Union of shipping to Cuba rockets capable of carrying nuclear warheads and of building launching pads for them, the Communist satellite regime was calling such indictments "slander and fabrication." "An egregious assertion," wrote *Rude Pravo* [the official newspaper of the Communist Party of Czechoslovakia] on Oct. 25 [1962], "a bubble that will burst the moment it is confronted with universally known facts." "Everyone knows," it continued the next day, and in its wake the radio and the remainder of the press, "that neither do any Soviet military installations exist in Cuba, nor are any being built."

But on Saturday, Oct. 27, Khrushchev admitted the "universally known facts." What could the propagandists do? That evening, hours after the public admission, Radio Prague's commentator elected to quote from the previous day's Soviet newspapers *Sovietskaja Rossija* and *Pravda*, and the *London Daily Worker*, calling Kennedy's assertions "an outright lie" and "falsifications of the American defense department."

[Soviet Press Agency Tass director] N.G. Palgunov's brochure, which grew into the fundamental textbook and technical guide for all Communist news agencies, gave no practical help for such emergencies. . . .

Being Politically Correct

Antonia Buzek, former managing foreign editor of Ceteka, the official Czechoslovak news agency, wrote in *Forum* in March 1962, after seeking asylum in London: "Whenever it appears that a particular news item may be of no use as propaganda but, because of its importance must nevertheless be printed, it . . . must be 'adjusted.' . . .

In practice, almost all news must be slanted, adapted to the party line. . . ."

Reporters, subeditors, editors, and heads of the propaganda agency, Mr. Buzek said, have a horror of a political error. They sometimes shift responsibility right up to the Prime Minister himself. "No newspaper in Czechoslovakia ever publishes any important piece of home or foreign news on its own"; each waits, he adds, for Ceteka as Ceteka waits for Tass. The Cuban crisis caught this unwieldy apparatus in a comedy of contradictions.

> 'The college man sitting in the chair of the President of the United States of America has, as the representative of aggressive forces, gone even further than Hitler.'

President Kennedy's dramatic disclosure of Oct. 22 came to the Czech propagandists as an immense surprise. On Oct. 20, the press was still announcing "tourist excursions" to Cuba. Without word from Tass, Radio Prague could only take Mr. Kennedy's speech as "being exaggerated . . . its purpose smells of propaganda and an effort to exert pressure." The radio comment of the 22nd was entirely in terms of "economic, political, and psychological pressure," with no hint of military danger.

While waiting for Tass, Prague did not even construe the announced arms blockade as aggression. Neither the government's declaration of Oct. 23, nor the simultaneous "spontaneous declaration of all the workers" to fulfill all commitments to Cuba mentioned either military aid or further arms shipments.

An Anti-Kennedy Tirade

On Oct. 24, *Rude Pravo* discovered Mr. Kennedy's "arrogance," spoke of his "swindle," and warned the world that "all freedoms are threatened." By the 25th, it had really gathered momentum: "The college man sitting in the chair of the President of the United States of America

Radio Prague started its coverage of the 1962 missile crisis with comparisons of President John F. Kennedy to Adolf Hitler, who is seen in this Czech newspaper from 1939. But that tone shifted as the event unfolded. (**AP Images.**)

has, as the representative of aggressive forces, gone even further than Hitler."

That evening on Radio Prague, a dispatch from New York correspondent Karen Kynel described the response to the crisis in the United States: "The only thing printed supporting the policy of the Kennedy administration was distributed by 12 youngsters posted outside the entrance to an office here in New York. . . . These were leaflets issued by the American Nazi party."

The commentator of the Prague "Chat" on the 24th linked what the station had been calling "Kennedy's stupid announcement" with the expectation of a new crisis in Berlin: "A really very probable connection does seem to exist. . . . First of all, Berlin would be militarily indefensible for the West, and, secondly, the signing of a peace treaty is certain to mean the utter defeat of American military policy in Europe."

But Khrushchev did not retaliate in Berlin. Instead, on Saturday the 27th, he admitted the presence of Soviet rockets in Cuba. The Czech propaganda could not find its balance all through that day. That night, Radio Prague began to allude to the need to work out an exchange of the base in Cuba for the bases in Turkey—the first mention, in passing, of the fact of missiles in Cuba.

A Surge of Patriotism, Praise, and Morality

The press took refuge the next day behind autumnal sentimentality, superior patriotism, rage. "This Sunday seems like any other," *Rude Pravo*'s lead article began. "Time passes as it usually does . . . yet once again we're an experience richer. . . . Once again, and all the more vividly . . . we have seen with what unconcealed ruthlessness, with what Hitler-like arrogance those gentlemen in their dinner jackets and generals' and admirals' uniforms are capable of whipping up action against the peace of the world. . . ."

Of Khrushchev and his rockets? In calm tones, the article proceeds: "A further significant step was taken on Saturday by the Soviet Government . . . the proposals of the Soviet Union are equable, reasonable, and realistic . . . they give the world cause for hope. . . ." The regime does not have to explain or justify, only tell the people how to obey: "On this autumn Sunday . . . we're aware of what is happening. We understand the chain of events. . . . Our response is calm. . . . Our people is a single voice and single power. . . ."

Where it had no facts, the press hid behind morality. It exhorted "citizenly demeanor," "steadfastness," "discretion." And *Rude Pravo*'s "Sunday Supplement For Children" tells the following child's tale in an article headed "Hands Off Cuba, Kennedy!"

> 'Cuba's future does not depend as much upon the Soviet Union as it does upon the peaceful intentions of the United States.'

"Do you know, dear children, what an American blockade of Cuba can do? It can cause the slow-down of production and the over-all shortage of raw materials and machinery; a lack of proper clothing, food, medicine—and even of school supplies. And that's not all. If Cuba were not to have sufficient defenses, any aggressive state could attack and destroy it . . . the U.S.S.R. would not abandon Cuba in its hour of need. You children have already read in your history books about how the valiant, courageous Soviet Union and its people defeated Hitler and liberated many lands—including Czechoslovakia—from him. . . . So don't worry, children. The Americans will have to retreat from the Caribbean!"

A Change of Tune

But on Oct. 29, the warlike tone fades. The Kennedy who was Hitler, Nero, Mussolini, must now be seen as the one on whom peace depends. Radio Prague's "Chat" that night encourages negotiations, since "Cuba's future does not depend as much upon the Soviet Union as it does upon the peaceful intentions of the United States." On Nov. 4, *Rude Pravo* is extolling "the viewpoint of international law and logic." By Nov. 11, Radio Bratislava is not only talking about capitalistic and socialistic systems living side by side in peace, but also "some kind of collaboration." Within two weeks, the propaganda apparatus has managed to take nearly every historic attitude toward the West.

Did the people manage to follow these gyrations? Cuba has never been popular in Czechoslovakia. Students were shouting: "Prague's breadlines lengthen that Havana's may shorten!" and "Cuba sí—meat no!" on May Day of 1962. On Oct. 28, Prague's evening paper *Vecerni Praha* described those who "dodged the demonstrations in order to rush off to get to the stores before anyone else. . . . Just what sort of frontline fighters are these? Do they expect to fight against international piracy by buying tins of cooking oil or cartons of salt? What do these people really believe in? . . . In the weight of hoarded provisions or in the power of our side?"

To stoke the revolutionary fires, *Rude Pravo* of Oct. 28 printed a description of a military review in Cardenas, Cuba, by Milena Honzikova, one of the Czech "tourists" there. Thus the Czech propagandists strove very hard to be, as Palgunov put it, "fighting and persuasive"; docile to Tass; morally superior to the West; and unruffled by the sudden jutting of facts from behind the arranged curtains. It was a critical and historic week.

CHAPTER 2

Controversies Surrounding the Cuban Missile Crisis

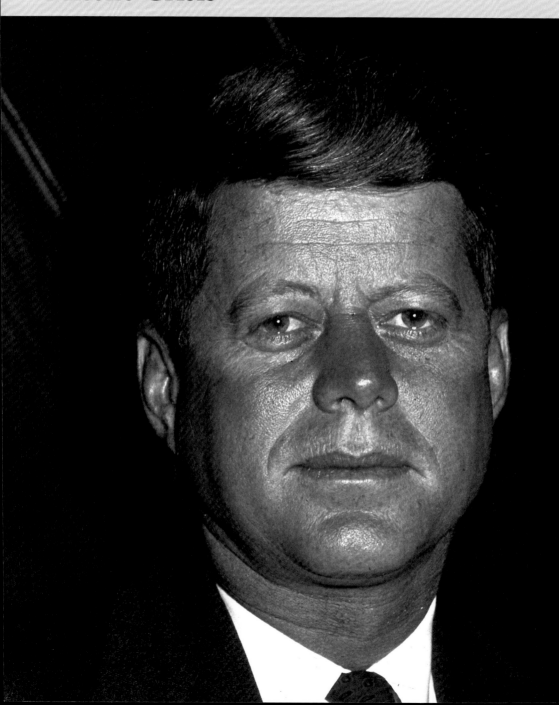

The Soviets Have Placed Offensive Weapons in Cuba

John F. Kennedy

In this October 22, 1962, address to the people of the United States, President John F. Kennedy announces that the United States has proof that the Soviet Union has begun a rapid offensive arms buildup in Cuba. He declares that the missile bases being built in Cuba will provide the Soviet Union a nuclear strike capability against the West. The range of some missiles will enable them to strike most of the major cities in the Western Hemisphere. Furthermore, the Soviets have made false statements, maintaining they do not need missile sites beyond the boundaries of the Soviet Union and that they are only helping Cuba strengthen its defense capabilities. Kennedy states that the United States cannot accept the Soviet lies or its clandestine decision to place strategic weapons outside of its own soil for the first time. John F. Kennedy served as president of the United States from 1961 to 1963.

Photo on previous page: John F. Kennedy's storied presidency draws much of its prominence from the Cuban missile crisis. (AP Images.)

SOURCE. John F. Kennedy, "The World on the Brink: John F. Kennedy and the Cuban Missile Crisis," *John F. Kennedy Presidential Library & Museum*, October 22, 1962.

This Government, as promised, has maintained the closest surveillance of the Soviet Military buildup on the island of Cuba. Within the past week, unmistakable evidence has established the fact that a series of offensive missile sites is now in preparation on that imprisoned island. The purpose of these bases can be none other than to provide a nuclear strike capability against the Western Hemisphere.

Upon receiving the first preliminary hard information of this nature last Tuesday morning [October 16] at 9 A.M., I directed that our surveillance be stepped up.

Initially, Soviet foreign minister Andrei Gromyko (right) assured President John F. Kennedy (left) that the USSR had only contributed to "the defense capabilities of Cuba." (Joseph Scherschel/Time Life Pictures/Getty Images.)

And having now confirmed and completed our evaluation of the evidence and our decision on a course of action, this Government feels obliged to report this new crisis to you in fullest detail.

Missiles and Bases: A Threat to Peace and Security

The characteristics of these new missile sites indicate two distinct types of installations. Several of them include medium range ballistic missiles capable of carrying a nuclear warhead for a distance of more than 1,000 nautical miles. Each of these missiles, in short, is capable of striking Washington, D.C., the Panama Canal, Cape Canaveral, Mexico City, or any other city in the southeastern part of the United States, in Central America, or in the Caribbean area.

Additional sites not yet completed appear to be designed for intermediate range ballistic missiles—capable of traveling more than twice as far—and thus capable of striking most of the major cities in the Western Hemisphere, ranging as far north as Hudson Bay, Canada, and as far south as Lima, Peru. In addition, jet bombers, capable of carrying nuclear weapons, are now being uncrated and assembled in Cuba, while the necessary air bases are being prepared.

This urgent transformation of Cuba into an important strategic base—by the presence of these large, long range, and clearly offensive weapons of sudden mass destruction—constitutes an explicit threat to the peace and security of all the Americas, in flagrant and deliberate defiance of the Rio Pact of 1947, the traditions of this Nation and hemisphere, the joint resolution of the 87th Congress, the Charter of the United Nations, and my own public warnings to the Soviets on September 4 and 13. This action also contradicts the repeated assurances of Soviet spokesmen, both publicly and privately delivered, that the arms buildup in Cuba would retain its original defensive character, and that the Soviet Union had no need or desire to station strategic missiles on the territory of any other nation.

Offensive Threats and False Statements

The size of this undertaking makes clear that it has been planned for some months. Yet only last month, after I had made clear the distinction between any introduction of ground-to-ground missiles and the existence of defensive antiaircraft missiles, the Soviet Government publicly stated on September 11, and I quote, "the armaments and military equipment sent to Cuba are designed exclusively for defensive purposes," that, and I quote the Soviet Government, "there is no need for the Soviet Government to shift its weapons . . . for a retaliatory

Profile: John Fitzgerald Kennedy

John Fitzgerald Kennedy was born May 29, 1917, to a wealthy and politically influential Massachusetts family. His father, Joseph P. Kennedy, was the first chairman of the U.S. Securities and Exchange Commission and ambassador to Great Britain from 1937 to 1940.

Plagued by illnesses during his childhood years, Kennedy entered Harvard University in 1936. He graduated cum laude in 1940. That same year, his book *Why England Slept* was published. Based on a thesis he wrote during his senior year, it examined Britain's delayed rearmament prior to World War II.

In 1941, with World War II raging in Europe, Kennedy enlisted in the Navy. For a time, he served as an intelligence officer in Washington, D.C. In late 1942, almost a year after he had requested sea duty, he was assigned to duty on PT (patrol torpedo) boats—small, fast boats used to attack larger ships. In August of the following year, Kennedy was serving on PT-109 in the South Pacific when it was rammed by a Japanese destroyer, slicing it into two pieces and killing two crewmen. The actions Kennedy took to rescue the surviving crew members won him a decoration for heroism and fame as a war hero.

blow to any other country, for instance Cuba," and that, and I quote their government, "the Soviet Union has so powerful rockets to carry these nuclear warheads that there is no need to search for sites for them beyond the boundaries of the Soviet Union." That statement was false.

Only last Thursday, as evidence of this rapid offensive buildup was already in my hand, Soviet Foreign Minister [Andrei] Gromyko told me in my office that he was instructed to make it clear once again, as he said his government had already done, that Soviet assistance to Cuba, and I quote, "pursued solely the purpose of contributing to the defense capabilities of Cuba," that, and I quote him, "training by Soviet specialists of Cuban nationals in handling defensive armaments was by no

In 1946, Kennedy's political career began in earnest when he ran for and won a seat in the U.S. House of Representatives. He remained in the House until 1953, when he began his first term in the U.S. Senate. That same year, he married Jacqueline Lee Bouvier, the daughter of a New York City financier. Four years later he won the Pulitzer Prize in biography for his 1956 book, *Profiles in Courage*, which described important decisions in the lives of eight U.S. senators.

In 1960, after a hard-fought campaign and by a very narrow margin, John Kennedy became the thirty-fifth president of the United States. He was the youngest man ever elected president, the first Roman Catholic to hold that office, and the first U.S. president born in the twentieth century. In his inaugural speech, he challenged Americans to play an active part in his New Frontier, urging them to "ask not what your country can do for you—ask what you can do for your country."

Kennedy's presidency was short-lived—only about one thousand days. While riding in a motorcade in Dallas, Texas, in November 1963, he fell victim to sniper bullets. Despite studies and investigations, his assassination has never been completely resolved.

means offensive, and if it were otherwise," Mr. Gromyko went on, "the Soviet Government would never become involved in rendering such assistance." That statement also was false.

Neither the United States of America nor the world community of nations can tolerate deliberate deception and offensive threats on the part of any nation, large or small. We no longer live in a world where only the actual firing of weapons represents a sufficient challenge to a nation's security to constitute maximum peril. Nuclear weapons are so destructive and ballistic missiles are so swift, that any substantially increased possibility of their use or any sudden change in their deployment may well be regarded as a definite threat to peace.

An Unacceptable and Aggressive Act

For many years both the Soviet Union and the United States, recognizing this fact, have deployed strategic nuclear weapons with great care, never upsetting the precarious status quo which insured that these weapons would not be used in the absence of some vital challenge. Our own strategic missiles have never been transferred to the territory of any other nation under a cloak of secrecy and deception; and our history—unlike that of the Soviets since the end of World War II—demonstrates that we have no desire to dominate or conquer any other nation or impose our system upon its people. Nevertheless, American citizens have become adjusted to living daily on the Bull's-eye of Soviet missiles located inside the U.S.S.R. or in submarines.

In that sense, missiles in Cuba add to an already clear and present danger. . . .

But this secret, swift, and extraordinary buildup of Communist missiles—in an area well known to have a special and historical relationship to the United States and the nations of the Western Hemisphere, in violation of Soviet assurances, and in defiance of American and hemispheric policy—this sudden, clandestine decision to station strategic weapons for the first time outside of Soviet soil—is a deliberately provocative and unjustified change in the status quo which cannot be accepted by this country. . . .

To halt this offensive buildup, a strict quarantine on all offensive military equipment under shipment to Cuba is being initiated. All ships of any kind bound for Cuba from whatever nation, or port will, if found to contain cargoes of offensive weapons, be turned back. . . .

I call upon [Soviet] Chairman [Nikita] Khrushchev to halt and eliminate this clandestine, reckless, and provocative threat to world peace and to stable relations between our two nations. . . . He has an opportunity now to move the world back from the abyss of destruction—by returning to his government's own words that it had no need to station missiles outside its own territory, and withdrawing these weapons from Cuba—by refraining from any action which will widen or deepen the present crisis—and then by participating in a search for peaceful and permanent solutions.

The Soviets Have Placed Defensive Weapons in Cuba

Nikita Khrushchev

> In the following viewpoint, an excerpt of a letter dated October 26, 1962, Soviet leader Nikita Khrushchev assures U.S. president John F. Kennedy that he is mistaken in his belief that Soviet armaments in Cuba are offensive. Khrushchev contends that all weapons in Cuba are of a defensive nature, and Soviet ships bound for Cuba are not carrying any armaments at all. He alleges that the misunderstanding is a matter of interpretation; the U.S. and the Soviet Union simply have different definitions for different types of military equipment. According to Khrushchev, the Soviets want a peaceful coexistence, not war. Nikita Khrushchev served as Soviet premier from 1958 to 1964.

SOURCE. Nikita Khrushchev, *The Cuban Missile Crisis, 1962: A National Security Archive Documents Reader*. Providence, RI: The New Press, 1992. Copyright © 1992 by Laurence Chang and Peter Kornbluh. Reproduced by permission of the author.

I can see, Mr. President, that you also are not without a sense of anxiety for the fate of the world, not
without an understanding and correct assessment
of the nature of modern warfare and what war entails.
What good would a war do you? You threaten us with
war. But you well know that the very least you would get
in response would be what you had given us; you would
suffer the same consequences. And that must be clear to
us—people invested with authority, trust and responsibility. We must not succumb to light-headedness and petty
passions, regardless of whether elections are forthcoming
in one country or another. These are all transitory things,
but should war indeed break out, it would not be in our
power to contain or stop it, for such is the logic of war.
I have taken part in two wars, and I know that war ends
only when it has rolled through cities and villages, sow-
ing death and destruction everywhere.

The Same Armaments,
Different Interpretations

I assure you on behalf of the Soviet Government and the
Soviet people that your arguments regarding offensive
weapons in Cuba are utterly unfounded. From what you
have written me it is obvious that our interpretations on
this point are different, or rather that
we have different definitions for one
type of military means or another.
And indeed, the same types of armaments may in actuality have different
interpretations.

> Do you really think that all we
> spend our time on is transport-
> ing so-called offensive weapons,
> atomic and hydrogen bombs?

You are a military man, and I hope
you will understand me. Let us take a
simple cannon for instance. What
kind of a weapon is it—offensive
or defensive? A cannon is a defensive weapon if it is
set up to defend boundaries or a fortified area. But
when artillery is concentrated and supplemented by an

appropriate number of troops, then the same cannon will have become an offensive weapon, since they prepare and clear the way for infantry to advance. The same is true for nuclear missile weapons, for any type of these weapons.

You are mistaken if you think that any of our armaments in Cuba are offensive. However, let us not argue at this point. Evidently, I shall not be able to convince you. But I tell you: You, Mr. President, are a military man and you must understand: How can you possibly launch an offensive even if you have an enormous number of missiles of various ranges and power on your territory, using these weapons alone? These missiles are a means of annihilation and destruction. But it is impossible to launch an offensive by means of these missiles, even nuclear missiles of 100 megaton yield, because it is only people—troops—who can advance. Without people any weapons, whatever their power, cannot be offensive.

No Grounds to Launch an Offensive

How can you, therefore, give this completely wrong interpretation, which you are now giving, that some weapons in Cuba are offensive, as you say? All weapons there—and I assure you of this—are of a defensive nature; they are in Cuba solely for purposes of defense, and we have sent them to Cuba at the request of the Cuban Government. And you say that they are offensive weapons.

But, Mr. President, do you really seriously think that Cuba could launch an offensive upon the United States and that even we, together with Cuba, could advance against you from Cuban territory? Do you really think so? How can that be? We do not understand. Surely, there has not been any such new development in military strategy that would lead one to believe that it is possible to advance that way. And I mean advance, not destroy; for those who destroy are barbarians, people who have lost their sanity.

I hold that you have no grounds to think so. You may regard us with distrust, but you can at any rate rest assured that we are of sound mind and understand perfectly well that if we launch an offensive against you, you will respond in kind. But you too will get in response whatever you throw at us. And I think you understand that too. . . .

The Soviet Goal—Peaceful Coexistence

This indicates that we are sane people, that we understand and assess the situation correctly. How could we, then, allow [ourselves] the wrong actions which you ascribe to us? Only lunatics or suicides, who themselves want to perish and before they die destroy the world, could do this. But we want to live and by no means do we want to destroy your country. We want something quite different: to compete with your country in a peaceful endeavor. We argue with you; we have differences on ideological questions. But our concept of the world is that questions of ideology, as well as economic problems, should be settled by other than military means; they must be solved in peaceful contest, or as this is interpreted in capitalist society—by competition. Our premise has been and remains that peaceful coexistence, of two different sociopolitical systems—a reality of our world—is essential, and that it is essential to ensure lasting peace. These are the principles to which we adhere.

An Unnecessary and Lawless Quarantine

You have now declared piratical measures, the kind that were practiced in the Middle Ages when ships passing through international waters were attacked, and you have called this a "quarantine" around Cuba. Our vessels will probably soon enter the zone patrolled by your Navy. I assure you that the vessels which are now headed for Cuba are carrying the most innocuous peaceful car-

Soviet premier Nikita Khrushchev sent missiles to Cuba but insisted that the USSR's differences with the United States "be settled by other than military means." (AFP/Getty Images.)

goes. Do you really think that all we spend our time on is transporting so-called offensive weapons, atomic and hydrogen bombs? Even though your military people may possibly imagine that these are some special kind of weapons, I assure you that they are the most ordinary kind of peaceful goods.

Therefore, Mr. President, let us show good sense. I assure you that the ships bound for Cuba are carrying no armaments at all. The armaments needed for the defense of Cuba are already there. I do not mean to say that there have been no shipments of armaments at all. No, there were such shipments. But now Cuba has already obtained the necessary weapons for defense.

I do not know whether you can understand me and believe me. But I wish you would believe yourself and agree that one should not give way to one's passions; that one should be master of them. And what direction are events taking now? If you begin stopping vessels it would be piracy, as you yourself know. If we should start doing this to your ship you would be just as indignant as we and the whole world are now indignant. Such actions cannot be interpreted otherwise, because lawlessness cannot be legalized. Were this allowed to happen then there would be no peace; nor would there be peaceful coexistence.

The United States Had No Policy or Firm Plan to Invade Cuba

Raymond L. Garthoff

In the following viewpoint taken from his 1989 book *Reflections on the Cuban Missile Crisis*, Raymond L. Garthoff acknowledges that in 1961 and 1962, the United States drew up military contingency plans for a possible air attack and invasion of Cuba. He maintains that Soviet leaders concluded that the United States had a policy and firm plan for U.S. armed forces to invade Cuba. Garthoff contends that the Soviets were mistaken. The United States had no firm political decision or intention to invade Cuba before the Cuban missile crisis exploded. Raymond L. Garthoff is a specialist on arms control, the Cold War, and the Soviet Union, and is the author of numerous books. During the Cuban missile crisis, he held the position of Special Assistant for the Soviet Bloc in the U.S. Department of State, Bureau of Political-Military Affairs.

SOURCE. Raymond L. Garthoff, *Reflections on the Cuban Missile Crisis*, rev. ed. Washington, D.C.: The Brookings Institution, 1989. Copyright © 1989 The Brookings Institution. Reproduced by permission.

S oviet accounts of the "Caribbean crisis" stress many indications that after the failure of the Bay of Pigs invasion in April 1961, the leaders of the United States continued to seek ways to remove Fidel Castro and communism from Cuba. That is generally true. Most such accounts, however, while more or less correctly noting various U.S. political, covert, and military actions in 1961–62, incorrectly conclude from that evidence that there was a policy and firm plan for a new invasion of Cuba by the United States' armed forces. Military contingency plans were prepared in 1961–62 for possible air attack and invasion, and under some circumstances, never precisely determined, there might have been an attack. But there was *no* firm American political decision or intention to invade Cuba before the crisis erupted in October 1962.

Amphibious U.S. military exercises—similar to those depicted here in the Philippines—may have misled the Soviets about American intentions in Vieques in 1962. (**AP Images.**)

Two Significant U.S. Military Exercises

The United States did conduct a series of large-scale military exercises in the Caribbean in the spring, summer, and fall of 1962. Between April 9 and 24, a major Marine air-ground task force carried out an amphibious exercise, *Lantphibex 1-62*, with an assault on the island of Vieques. Exercise *Quick Kick* from April 19 to May 11 along the U.S. southeastern coast involved 79 ships, 300 aircraft, and more than 40,000 troops. While publicly announced, the fact that it was designed to test an actual CINCLANT (Commander-in-Chief, Atlantic) contingency plan against Cuba was not of course disclosed. The Soviets and Cubans, however, correctly assumed that it was testing a war plan. These U.S. exercises in April and May were highly significant because that was the period when the Soviet leaders were considering and making

Profile: Fidel Alejandro Castro Ruz

Fidel Castro ruled Cuba for almost 50 years. A revolutionary for most of his life, he was born on his father's sugarcane plantation in Cuba on August 13, 1926. He received his early education in Jesuit schools. In 1945, he entered the University of Havana, where he became a student leader and political activist.

After graduating in 1950 with a law degree, Castro set up a private law practice in Havana. Two years later, he ran for Congress. The elections, however, never took place because of a successful military coup led by Fulgencio Batista to take over the Cuban government. Castro tried unsuc-

cessfully through legal means to have Batista removed from power. He then took matters into his own hands. In 1953, he organized a group of rebels and led an attack on military barracks in Santiago. The attack failed, and he and others received fifteen-year prison sentences.

Released after two years in prison, he and his supporters headed to Mexico, where they organized a revolutionary force called the 26th of July Movement. Castro returned to Cuba and in 1956, initiated guerrilla war against the Batista government. It took almost three years, but Castro and his followers finally man-

important decisions about expanded military support for Cuba, including the decision to deploy Soviet missiles. Later Soviet accounts charged that these exercises were part of the preparation for further direct U.S. military action against Cuba under an October 1961 directive from President [John F.] Kennedy to the Joint Chiefs of Staff to draw up plans for an invasion of Cuba. This was a distorted perception, because the plans were contingency plans, *not* plans adopted in pursuance of a decision to invade. Nonetheless, they seemed to Cuban and Soviet intelligence analysts and leaders to reflect a firm intention, or at the least an active hostility with probable intent.

Operation Mongoose

Apart from overt military activities, the Kennedy administration was also responsible after November 30, 1961,

aged to overthrow Batista and send him into exile. Years later Castro said, "I began revolution with 82 men. If I had to do it again, I [would] do it with 10 or 15 and absolute faith. It does not matter how small you are if you have faith and plan of action."

Castro was named prime minister of Cuba, a title he held until 1976, when he became president. He had almost total power. Early on, he turned Cuba toward communism. In 1965, he merged Cuba's Communist Party with his revolutionary organizations and made himself head of the Cuban Communist Party, Cuba's only politi-

cal party to this day. In 1998, Castro, running unopposed, was elected to his fifth term as president of Cuba.

Under Castro, thousands of new schools were opened, the literacy rate climbed to 98 percent, and a universal health care system was put in place. At the same time, however, Castro kept tight control, retaliating against all those who opposed his government and carving away bit by bit at civil liberties. He maintained control until February 19, 2008, when, at the age of 81 and citing poor health, he resigned as president of Cuba and military commander-in-chief.

for sending sabotage and diversionary units of Cuban emigrés on raids into Cuba under a covert action plan called "Operation Mongoose," and even for plotting to kill Castro. Between late 1961 and August 1962, the main focus of actual operations was on intelligence infiltration, but other actions were also undertaken. A recently declassified Mongoose planning document of February 20, 1962, projected a program and timetable culminating in a wide popular revolt in Cuba, a, development that in turn was expected both to require and to justify American military intervention, in October 1962. Submitted by Brigadier General Edward Lansdale, the Mongoose chief of operations, the projected program was, however, not accepted by the administration, which at that time approved only the intelligence infiltration stage of the plan. Moreover, the approved guidelines, issued on March 14, while recognizing that "final success [in overthrowing the Castro regime] will require decisive U.S. military intervention," authorized only covert operations "short of those reasonably calculated to inspire a revolt within the target area, or other development which would require U.S. armed intervention." Cuban and Soviet intelligence were, however, aware that the U.S. government was undertaking a concerted covert action program aimed at overthrowing the Castro regime.

> It was . . . not unreasonable for Cuban and Soviet leaders to be concerned in 1962 over intensified U.S. hostile action against Cuba, including the possibility of an invasion.

Additional U.S. Operations Against Cuba

The United States also aggressively pursued a wide range of overt political and economic maneuvers against the Castro regime. In January 1962 at Punta del Este, Uruguay, the United States succeeded in gaining enough Latin American votes to suspend Cuba from membership in the Organization of American States (OAS). By the spring of that year, some fifteen Latin American countries (although not the several largest) had followed the earlier American lead and broken diplomatic relations with Cuba. Soviet officials and commentators have described the exclusion of Cuba from the OAS as the "diplomatic preparation" for invasion.

The United States also pressed economic warfare against Cuba. The restrictions on U.S. trade with Cuba established in 1960 and 1961 were expanded to a complete embargo on February 3, 1962. The ban on trade carried in American ships was later expanded to deny entry to U.S. ports to ships of other countries en route to or from Cuba. And behind the scenes the United States used diplomatic means in the first half of 1962 to frustrate Cuban trade negotiations with Israel, Jordan, Iran, Greece, and Japan.

In short, by the spring of 1962 the United States had embarked on a concerted campaign of overt and covert political, economic, psychological, and clandestine operations to weaken the Castro regime. A covert destabilization operations program was under way, including attempts to assassinate Castro. Military contingency plans for air attack and invasion of Cuba had been drawn up, and a series of military exercises training for possible execution of those plans was taking place.

It was thus not unreasonable for Cuban and Soviet leaders to be concerned in 1962 over intensified U.S. hostile action against Cuba, including the possibility of an invasion. There had not, however, been any decision by President Kennedy to invade Cuba or to overthrow the Castro regime if nonmilitary means failed to topple it. That was the situation in April–May 1962 when the Soviet and Cuban leadership began to consider more far-reaching measures of Soviet military assistance to Cuba.

The Soviets Put Missiles in Cuba to Alter Perceptions of the Balance of Power

Ray S. Cline

In this 1989 magazine article, Roy S. Cline argues that the Soviets did not put missiles in Cuba to defend the government of Cuban revolutionary leader Fidel Castro from the Americans. Cline contends that declarations to that effect should be viewed as no more than an attempt to revise history. The Soviet Union would sacrifice the countries that depended on it politically if protecting them meant risking nuclear damage to the homeland. Soviet leader Nikita Khrushchev had a broader strategic goal in mind than defense: altering the global balance of power. Ray S. Cline served as Deputy Director for Intelligence for the Central Intelligence Agency in 1962 and played a major role in the Cuban missile crisis. He is director of the Center for Strategic and

SOURCE. Ray S. Cline, "Commentary: The Cuban Missile Crisis," *Foreign Affairs*, vol. 68, Fall 1989, pp. 190–91, 193–96. Copyright © 1989 by the Council on Foreign Relations, Inc. Reproduced by permission of the author's estate.

International Studies at Georgetown University in Washington, D.C., the author of numerous books, and the founder of the D.C.-based United States Global Strategy Council.

I n Washington, crucial facts are commonly observed disappearing down the historical "memory hole." Recollections of the Cuban missile crisis of 1962 are in fashion now. Naturally, dim recollections and diverse perceptions cloud the picture, but more than that there appears to be a genial wish on the part of many of the reminiscing original participants in the "Thirteen Days in October" to demonstrate fairness and balanced judgment about the Soviet Union, deferring politely to what Soviet officials are saying in this extraordinary age of selective *glasnost* [policy of openness].

History Revised

One thing is clear to me, one of the aging participants who remembers the 1962 crisis pretty clearly. [Soviet leader] Mikhail Gorbachev's team of official intellectuals is engaged in a program of historical revisionism serving Moscow's interest. Some of the facts being laid out are misleading or simply not true, and the geopolitical thrust of the Soviet interpretation of history is false. . . .

As Gorbachev's policy interest changes, . . . the past is being substantially revised. It is not necessary, however, for Americans to believe everything they are told or to forget what they thought they knew.

The thrust of the Soviet argument at a two-day U.S.-Soviet-Cuban symposium held in Moscow January 27–28, 1989, was that [Soviet premier Nikita] Khrushchev feared an American invasion of Cuba and made the extraordinary strategic move of attempting to place missiles on Cuban soil to defend his protégé, Fidel Castro. Many of the Americans attending the symposium, including former Secretary of Defense Robert McNamara and former Assistant to the President for National Security Affairs McGeorge Bundy, reacted to these reminiscences in the company of Soviet and Cuban speakers by tending to accept that Khrushchev may have acted defensively. They seemed rather to like the romantic idea that the two superpowers were at the very brink of war, as Gorbachev urged them to believe. But in my view neither of these propositions is valid. I certainly doubt they are the heart of the matter.

The truth is that both sides were scrupulous in avoiding even the remote chance of an actual nuclear exchange, for the simple reason that, as we all assured President [John F.] Kennedy, the United States had at least a four-to-one advantage in ICBMs [intercontinental ballistic missiles] and a much greater superiority in nuclear weapons capability, as well as a much greater number of bomber aircraft of intercontinental range. . . .

> The aim was not to defend Castro but to alter the psychological and political perceptions of the balance of power, particularly in Washington.

My reservations about the symposium in Moscow go even deeper than specific questions of the presence of nuclear warheads in Cuba. The most dubious proposition advanced in these discussions was that protecting Castro's socialist state as a symbol of Soviet political power in the Caribbean was Khrushchev's primary motive, and that he was forced into it by Kennedy's intention to mount a military invasion of Cuba.

Undoubtedly, Moscow has gained many advantages from Cuba in intelligence collection and power projection in Latin America, and it is clear that Khrushchev decided to give a lot of military help to Castro when they met during the U.N. General Assembly session in New York in 1960. Nobody qualified to judge has ever suggested, however, that any incumbent group of Soviet party leaders would expose the homeland of the Soviet Union to a serious risk of extensive nuclear damage in order to save an asset in a distant part of the world. Even to this day Moscow has never included Cuba in the Warsaw Pact or any formal military alliance, despite repeated requests from Castro to be admitted to the inner club. Leninism [a political theory of dictatorship] as taught in the party schools cries out against any suggestion that the Soviet motherland should suffer to protect a client state, preferring to retreat from danger so as to live to fight another day in better circumstances. History repeatedly reveals that Moscow follows this principle, sacrificing political dependencies as necessary. . . . Gorbachev still emulates [Vladimir] Lenin and is undoubtedly even now following this policy of prudent withdrawals aimed at strengthening the centralized control system.

Altering the Balance of Power

I am convinced that Khrushchev had a broader strategic goal in mind in 1962, with the endgame focusing on Berlin. Khrushchev knew the deployment would cause a worldwide political storm, but evidently thought Kennedy would simply be obliged to get used to the idea of having missiles in substantial numbers pointed at the United States. Unlike Bundy and McNamara, I agree with what I understand to be the views of [Raymond L.] Garthoff [State Department political-military analyst] and Paul Nitze, a perennial sage on Soviet behavior, that the aim was not to defend Castro but to alter the psychological and political perceptions of the balance of power, particularly in Washington. I am sure the impact on American thinking would have been shattering if we had not detected the missiles before they were deployed and recognized how deliberately Khrushchev had tried to deceive Kennedy with his misleading statements about offensive weapons in the summer of 1962.

In any case, Khrushchev was not crazy enough to fire the missiles, although he was a great braggart about the

> Plainly Khrushchev's game was strategic blackmail, using Cuba to alter what Soviet theorists call the 'correlation of forces.'

destructiveness of his military weapons. He surely meant to shock world opinion into thinking he had got the whip hand over the United States by his unprecedented and menacing deployment of missiles to Cuba. After all, 42 missiles, the number actually delivered to Cuba, would have doubled the total first-strike capability available to the Soviet Union in the fall of 1962.

The Issue of Berlin

Having immobilized Kennedy from resort to nuclear retaliation as a result of this sudden jump to missile parity, Khrushchev then would have tried to cash in his chips in Berlin. He probably hoped to whipsaw the NATO [North Atlantic Treaty Organization] powers into negotiating a strategic retreat rather than face the uncertain consequences of a conventional military conflict in Europe. Against the backdrop of a sudden nuclear scare, it might have worked, especially as there were divergences among the European allies about the price to be paid for Berlin.

Even before the Cuban crisis, there was substantial evidence already reported of Soviet diplomatic maneuvering and actual forward deployments of Soviet military units in Germany. All of this stopped dead on October 23, 1962. Plainly Khrushchev's game was strategic blackmail, using Cuba to alter what Soviet theorists call the "correlation of forces"—by which they mean a complex psychological, political and military assessment. In this way he could regain strategic momentum in Berlin, where Moscow had enormous advantages in mounting threats and conducting military operations. If Kennedy and his NATO partners had capitulated on Berlin, as some might have wished, the course of superpower relations in the 1960s and later decades would have been entirely different.

Khrushchev's mind worked in just such devious and conspiratorial ways. The best evidence that he had in mind a scheme larger than simply protecting his Caribbean investment is presented in a book recounting Soviet President Anastas Mikoyan's post-crisis visit to Washington. Janos Radvanyi, a Hungarian counselor of embassy in Washington and later a defector to the United States, reports that Mikoyan said at a Soviet embassy briefing for diplomats from communist countries on November 30, 1962, that the missile deployment in Cuba was intended not just to defend Castro but was also aimed at "achieving a definite shift in the power relationship between the socialist and the capitalist worlds." In this ideological context, something would have to happen in Europe to be of so great a benefit.

Former CIA deputy director Ray S. Cline saw the Soviets' key goal in placing missiles in Cuba as altering the balance of power—not shielding the Cubans. (Terry Ashe/Time Life Pictures/Getty Images.)

Khrushchev's Waning Prestige

The final point worth making is that Khrushchev was under heavy pressure at this time to do something to restore his prestige, in particular to fulfill his boasts and threats about changing the ground rules for Berlin. Kennedy had countered his threatening advances in Germany with firm statements and gestures of determination to defend Berlin. The United States also had revealed the CIA's findings from remote-sensing satellite imagery that the Soviet Union had only a few ICBMs, rather than the superior force Khrushchev had deceptively implied and the U.S. intelligence community had accepted until overhead imagery became available in 1962. Since his overblown claims of missile superiority had been exploded, Khrushchev badly needed a triumph in international affairs. The wisdom about this situation has been captured by Walt Rostow, then chief of the State Department Planning Group—including a reference to Cuba and, by chance, to me. Concerning the summer of 1962, Rostow wrote:

> The planning group over which I presided, representing the best minds in the second level of government . . . had the advantage of time to reflect at length on the meaning of the sharpening Soviet position on Berlin since the spring. . . . We had canvassed the possibilities of a convulsive effort by Khrushchev to retrieve his waning position. . . . As I recall, Ray Cline of the CIA was the most perceptive among us. I closed the meeting on August 21 by observing we might be about to see the greatest act of risk-taking since the war. Cline said: "Maybe we are seeing it right now in Cuba."

On this note, I rest my case on the real meaning of the Cuban crisis. Khrushchev did indeed take the gigantic risk of deploying missiles to Cuba in order to destabilize Germany and NATO, hoping thereby to alter perceptions of the relative strength of the two superpowers. We did not hear much of that in Moscow in January 1989. We ought to press Soviet officials to open up their archives as the United States has done, and not simply accept the simplistic Soviet message about Khrushchev defending Cuba against American military attack.

Washington had no plans to attack, as the approval of the strictly limited covert operations Mongoose plan plainly established. In my position [as deputy director for intelligence] at the CIA at the time, I was well informed about this operation. I can state with confidence that there was no basis in American policy for a Soviet fear of an American invasion of Cuba when Khrushchev was making his decision to base missiles there. Claims that these fears motivated Khrushchev represent a blatant case of historical revisionism to justify Khrushchev's dangerous gamble. He was ebullient, not frightened, in heading into the Cuban adventure.

Cultural Differences Helped Cause the Cuban Missile Crisis

Sergei Khrushchev

In this 2002 magazine article, Sergei Khrushchev asserts that cultural differences were a major cause of the Cuban missile crisis. Soviet leader Nikita Khrushchev and U.S. president John F. Kennedy each thought in terms of his own culture. As a result, both misjudged how their decisions would affect the other side. Khrushchev felt obligated to put missiles in Cuba for its defense and assumed Kennedy would not use them as a reason to attack the Soviet Union. Kennedy thought an aggressive Soviet Union had placed offensive nuclear weapons in Cuba to intimidate the United States and took steps to show the strategy would not work. The son of Soviet premier Nikita Khrushchev, Sergei Khrushchev has been a senior fellow at the Watson Institute for International Studies at Brown University since 1996. He has authored more than 250 books

SOURCE. Sergei Khrushchev, "How My Father and President Kennedy Saved the World," *American Heritage*, vol. 53, October 2002. Copyright © 2002 American Heritage Publishing. All rights reserved. Reproduced by permission of the publisher and the author.

and articles, including *Khrushchev on Khrushchev* (1990), and *Nikita Khrushchev: Crisis and Missiles* (1994).

The world came close to a nuclear clash three times during the half-century of the Cold War. The first was in Korea. . . .

The second time came in 1962, at the moment of greatest tension around Cuba, 45 years ago this October. And the last was in Vietnam. . . .

On the first and last occasions, American political leaders had a choice. But during the 13-day crisis of October 1962, events almost spun beyond control of either the White House or the Kremlin. Perhaps the most interesting aspect of the Cuban Missile Crisis is the fact that its causes were not solely what had become the familiar competition between two superpowers, America and Russia, but something more dangerous, the cultural difference—I would say differences in civilization—between them. Because of those differences, the leaders were unable to judge with any accuracy what effect their decisions would have on the other side.

Sergei Khrushchev argues that despite differences between the U.S. and Soviet leaders that led to the missile crisis, the American president and the Soviet premier both sought a peaceful outcome. (AP Images.)

However detailed the information the White House got from its intelligence sources and diplomats, the President based his final decision on his idea of conduct in the Kremlin. That is the crux of the matter. People invariably think in terms of their own traditions, their own culture, which may have nothing in common with the other party's way of thinking. Furthermore, a leader will trust his own intuition more than all the intelligence agencies in the world. Otherwise he would not be a leader.

Differences in civilization affect a country's vision not only of the future but of the past. Every country has its own historical mythology. The American mythology of the Cuban missile crisis is familiar: An aggressive Soviet Union, with the cooperation of a local dictator, Fidel Castro, placed offensive nuclear weapons, ballistic missiles, in Cuba, with the intention of cowing the United States. When President John F. Kennedy learned of this, he quite properly threatened the Soviet leader, Nikita Khrushchev, who "blinked" first and pulled his men and his missiles out of the island. The United States rightly won, and Khrushchev was soon swept from power.

But how did Cuba look from the windows of the Kremlin during the Cold War? At the beginning of 1959 the Soviet leaders could hardly imagine any fate that might link Moscow and Havana. No specialists in the Central Committee, much less Father, even knew much about Latin America. . . .

When Father asked for information about Cuba, it turned out there was none to give him. Neither the Communist Party Central Committee's International Department, KGB intelligence, nor military intelligence had any idea who Castro was or what he was fighting for. Father advised them to consult Cuba's Communists. . . .

> I asked Father repeatedly, 'How can we help Cuba?'

In 1960 Father decided to send his deputy Anastas Mikoyan to Cuba to discover what motivated Castro. . . .

He visited Father at the *dacha* on the eve of his departure, and I remember one small episode. A group of us went for a walk, and one of Father's aides reported on Castro's recent trip to Washington to meet President Eisenhower. No one had any reliable information. The aide tried to persuade the group that Castro was an American agent, or at least ready to dance to the White House's tune. You couldn't trust him: That was the Kremlin's view of Castro at the time.

Mikoyan returned from Cuba elated. He told Father in minute detail about his talks with the brothers Castro and other Cubans. In his opinion, they were honorable fighters for freedom and must be helped economically and politically. There was no talk yet of military assistance, and Father was cautious in evaluating Castro. Meanwhile, Washington continued to exert every effort to push the Cuban leader into the U.S.S.R.'s embrace. The economic blockade of Cuba announced by the United States was an important factor. It all began with sugar. To teach Castro a lesson, after he began to nationalize American petroleum refineries, the Americans stopped buying any sugar from Cuba. The Cubans had to look for a new customer. At first Father didn't believe we would be that customer, since Russia had its own sugar and had never bought any.

World prices for sugar soared after the embargo was announced, and Father made fun of the Americans, who would now have to drink "empty tea." But in fact Cuba's neighbors in the Caribbean increased their sugar production and supplied the Americans. Castro asked for help. We had to rescue our new friends. Father reluctantly approved the temporary purchase of Cuban sugar in exchange for Soviet fuel.

John Kennedy replaced Dwight Eisenhower in the White House in January 1961, as the situation in Cuba grew increasingly threatening. Bombs began to explode on the streets of Havana and claimed their first victims. I asked Father repeatedly, "How can we help Cuba?" He thought the most we could do was sell it weapons. I asked him: "Shouldn't we sign a mutual assistance treaty with Cuba, as we have with our European and Asian neighbors?" Father thought the idea not only useless but dangerous. If the Americans invaded Cuba, how could

Profile: Nikita Sergeyevich Khrushchev

Nikita Khrushchev was born in Kalinovka in southern Russia on April 17, 1894. At age fifteen he became an apprentice mechanic in Yuzovka. When his apprenticeship ended, he was employed as a machine repairman in coal mines of the region.

In 1918 Khrushchev joined the Communist Party, and he enrolled in the Red Army to fight in the civil war then in progress. After nearly three years of service, he returned to Yuzovka and was appointed assistant manager of a mine. Soon thereafter, he entered the Donets Industrial Institute, from which he graduated in 1925. He then took up his career as a full-time party official, beginning as secretary of a district party committee near Yuzovka.

Four years later Khrushchev attended the Industrial Academy in Moscow for training in industrial administration and left in 1931 to become secretary of a district party committee in Moscow. Within four years he became head of the party organization of Moscow.

In 1938 he was made first secretary of the Ukrainian Communist Party and was named to the Politburo, the ruling body of the Soviet Communist Party. Except for a short interval in 1947, he retained his authority until 1949.

we help the Cubans? The U.S. Navy was vastly superior to ours. Cuba was 90 miles by sea from Florida and 7,000 miles from the nearest Soviet port. What else could be done? Start a third world war? Insane. Father preferred not to take the risk. Instead he decided to speed up deliveries of small arms, tanks, and artillery—but not directly. Cuba signed an agreement with Czechoslovakia rather than the U.S.S.R.

Early on the morning of April 17, 1961, Father's sixty-sixth birthday, an invasion force landed at the Bay of Pigs in Cuba. Reports said that only Cuban émigrés took part in the operation and that the U.S. fleet cruising offshore was not interfering. Father didn't believe it. His mood turned grim. He nourished no illusions that Castro could withstand the Americans. Then Castro announced pub-

In 1949 Khrushchev was summoned to Moscow to serve in the party's secretariat. In 1953 Khrushchev was among the eight men in whose hands power became concentrated. Within a few months he became first secretary of the Central Committee of the Soviet Communist Party—that is, its chief official.

By 1955 he was the foremost political figure in the Soviet Union. Three years later, he became chairman of the Council of Ministers. In that role, he became the most powerful man in the country.

Khrushchev encouraged the policy of de-Stalinization. The Soviet Union's standard of living rose, intellectual and artistic life became somewhat freer, and the authority of the political police was reduced. In addition, relations with the outside world were generally improved, and Soviet prestige rose.

Khrushchev's fortunes eventually began to take a downward turn. Some of his ambitious economic projects failed, and his handling of foreign affairs resulted in a number of setbacks. In October 1964 party leaders united to require him to leave office. He died on September 11, 1971, in Moscow.

licly that he had chosen socialism. He resolved to win or die as a Communist. Father disapproved: "This isn't the time to do it. He's burning all the bridges behind him. Now the Americans won't let him off. There's no use thinking of negotiations." On the other hand, such dedication made a powerful impression on Father.

Hours passed. Days passed. Castro held on and even gradually seized the initiative. The Americans did not invade. At three-fifteen on the morning of April 20, Havana Radio announced that the mercenaries had been routed and the Cuban people were victorious. The battle had lasted 72 hours.

Father beamed. He sent heartfelt congratulations to his new friend Fidel. But he believed the Americans would not give up: They would take stock of their mistakes, choose their time, and then bring the weight of their regular army to bear.

The defense of Cuba became a matter of prestige for the Soviet Union, something like West Berlin was for the United States. If you did not defend that small patch of land deep inside enemy territory that was allied to you, no one would believe in your willingness or, more important, your ability to defend your allies. That was what motivated President Kennedy to proclaim himself a Berliner. But Kennedy had a big army in West Germany and NATO at his back.

> Who would dream that Kennedy was preparing to start a war, to precipitate a Russia barely reviving after the last war into a new cycle of destruction?

How would we help Cuba if the Americans took it into their heads to attack? Send our ships and planes? The Americans would block all access to the island whether by sea or air. The only resort was to do something extraordinary enough to make Washington understand that an assault on Cuba would have dire consequences.

At the end of May 1962, Father decided to send strategic nuclear missiles to Cuba. In making this decision, he relied on our Russian and European experience—on our history. For centuries enemies had constantly replaced one another on Russia's borders: the Mongols, Swedes, Poles; Lithuanians, Turks, Napoleon, the British, Germans, and again the Germans; after the Second World War the Germans had been replaced by U.S. air bases. American bombers could demolish our cities at any moment. During its entire history Russia had been within range of hostile weaponry. Russia had to rely on sound judgment on the part of opposing political leaders, on an American President's not sending his squadrons to bomb Moscow without good reason. Father assumed that Americans—not just the President but ordinary people—would think more or less the same way.

Who would dream that Kennedy was preparing to start a war, to precipitate a Russia barely reviving after the last war into a new cycle of destruction? And for what? For the victory of communism in the United States? Father often said that communism was not a dogma but a better, richer, freer life for ordinary people. Americans were a pragmatic people When they were convinced, sooner or later, of the advantages of the new system, they would choose it over capitalism, which was increasingly decrepit and convulsed by economic crisis. Why should we fight to achieve that goal when time was on social-ism's side? And how could Americans imagine that we would attack them when they enjoyed a 9 to 1 superiority in nuclear weapons? (At the time, the CIA even thought it was 18 to 1.)

> " It seemed to Americans that they could continue to live as before only if the missiles were removed from Cuba, and removed at any price. "

That was what Father supposed, but Americans thought otherwise. They were fortunate. For more than two centuries wide oceans had protected their land from enemies. Unlike Russians, they were used to living in security and were horrified by the possibility, however remote, of any vulnerability. The presence of Soviet ballistic missiles near America's borders evoked shock, and even psychosis. The press further inflamed emotions; the country lost its bearings; and the Cuban Missile Crisis became primarily an American psychological crisis. It seemed to Americans that they could continue to live as before only if the missiles were removed from Cuba, and removed at any price.

Neither Father in the Kremlin nor President Kennedy in the White House was prepared for such a turn of events. They had to look for a way out of the crisis while improvising on the run. President Kennedy could not for a moment agree to the presence of missiles on the island, even though he understood that the Soviet Union would use them only in case of the most extreme necessity, just as the United States would not launch the missiles it had long before deployed in Turkey, Italy, and Britain. If he allowed them to stay, Americans would accuse him of treachery and Congress would begin the process of impeachment. The missiles must be removed, but in such a way that he did not lose control of events and unintentionally start a nuclear war.

Father felt more or less the same way. The White House was unaware of the fact that in Cuba there were not only strategic missiles but also several dozen tactical missiles, also with nuclear warheads. If America invaded, the Soviet military on the island, under the pressure of the enemy's overwhelming force and faced with the choice of surrendering or unleashing nuclear strikes on the attackers, would surely choose the latter. This was even more likely since communications with Moscow, always unreliable, would probably cease altogether at the moment of attack. With the help of tactical nuclear weapons, Soviet forces . . . would undoubtedly repel the invasion, destroy the landing force, and sink American ships. But what then? It was not hard to imagine how the White House would react, and it was unlikely that the world would escape a major war.

The world was lucky. Neither President Kennedy nor Father stumbled. They resolved not to act rashly. . . .

The Cuban Missile Crisis was resolved. We survived, and I could write this article for the anniversary, and you can read it. But everything might have turned out differently. You, I, and all mankind might have disappeared from the face of the earth. The fact that this did not happen is the greatest achievement of those Cold War warriors President John F. Kennedy and my father, the premier of the Soviet Union, Nikita Khrushchev. Father said, more than once, "We differed from Kennedy in every respect. He defended his capitalist belief, his world, and we defended ours, our concept of justice. We had one thing in common: Both he and I did everything we could to preserve peace on earth."

Recklessness of U.S. and Soviet Leaders Helped Cause the Cuban Missile Crisis

John Swift

In this 2007 journal article, John Swift claims that both U.S. president John F. Kennedy and Soviet premier Nikita Khrushchev acted irresponsibly in bringing about the Cuban missile crisis. Khrushchev insisted not only on installing missiles in Cuba, but on doing so in secret. He should have realized that such action could not be kept secret long and that the United States would have reacted as it did. Kennedy let his distrust and dislike of Cuban president Fidel Castro take precedence over good sense and, instead of employing tact and diplomacy, permitted covert actions against Cuba. Although ultimately both Kennedy and Khrushchev acted responsibly and took pains to secure a peaceful resolution, Swift contends that their earlier actions and miscalculations could easily have resulted in nuclear disas-

SOURCE. John Swift, "The Cuban Missile Crisis," *History Review*, March 2007, pp. 6–11. Copyright © 2007 History Today Ltd. Reproduced by permission.

ter. John Swift is a Lecturer in History at St. Martin's College, Lancaster, UK, and the author of *The Palgrave Concise Historical Atlas of the Cold War.*

For 14 days in October 1962 the world stood on the brink of nuclear war. The Soviet Union had secretly stationed nuclear weapons on the island of Cuba, and when the government of the United States discovered them, and demanded their withdrawal, the most dangerous confrontation of the Cold War followed. A single miscalculation made either in the White House or the Kremlin could have precipitated catastrophe. How did this standoff arise? How did the Superpowers extricate themselves from it? Was anything learned from the crisis? Should any party be held more at fault than the other? . . .

Kennedy's Warnings, Khrushchev's Concerns

[U.S. president John F.] Kennedy . . . warned the Soviet Union against challenging the USA in the western hemisphere. Sending defensive weapons, such as surface to air missiles (SAMs), would be tolerated, surface to surface missiles, which carried nuclear warheads, would not. Perhaps more threateningly, in 1962 a large-scale military exercise was undertaken by US forces in the Caribbean, in which 40,000 military personnel practiced invading an unnamed island to overthrow a dictator threateningly codenamed Ortsac. Kennedy wanted to alarm [Cuban leader Fidel] Castro, and he succeeded. But he also alarmed Soviet leader Nikita Khrushchev.

The Soviet government had welcomed the Cuban revolution; and as American hostility to it grew, so did Soviet support. Cuba was never really an unquestioning servant of Moscow, but the state was growing increasingly dependent upon Moscow for military and eco-

nomic aid. In the aftermath of the Bay of Pigs [an unsuccessful attempt in 1961 by U.S.-backed Cuban exiles to overthrow the Castro government], Castro had declared his commitment to Communism for the first time. And in Moscow, as in Havana, there was a growing conviction that Kennedy was preparing to invade Cuba. As it was the only communist state in the western hemisphere, Khrushchev could not allow this.

Khrushchev also had other concerns. Since the launch of the Soviet satellite Sputnik 1 in October 1957, Khrushchev had proclaimed an entirely fictitious superiority in Intercontinental Ballistic Missiles (ICBMs). Kennedy had campaigned for the presidency proclaiming he would match the supposed Soviet advantage, closing the 'missile gap' as it was known. Even when he found that the strategic balance was, in real-

A U.S. destroyer (foreground) escorts a Soviet freighter loaded with nuclear missiles from Cuba back to the Soviet Union. The recklessness of Kennedy and of Khrushchev put the United States and the USSR on the path to a nuclear showdown. (Carl Mydans/ Time Life Pictures/Getty Images.)

ity, heavily in America's favour, Kennedy still ordered a major expansion of US ICBM forces. Khrushchev, who was desperate to divert resources from the military to domestic reform, was now caught by his own bluff and faced ruinous expense to fill a very real 'missile gap' that was in America's favour.

But American actions perhaps suggested a way out for Khrushchev. In 1962 American Jupiter missiles were stationed in Turkey, well within range of Soviet targets. Why not follow their example and station Intermediate Range and Medium Range Ballistic Missiles (IRBMs and MRBMs) in Cuba, where they could threaten most of the continental USA? This would be a cheap way to offset the American missile advantage, it would deter an American invasion of the island, it would be a proportional response to the missiles in Turkey, and it might make the United States more accommodating over other issues, such as Berlin.

> Khrushchev, in fact, had never considered that the presence of missiles in Cuba would be deemed a monstrous threat in the United States.

West Berlin was a western enclave deep in East Germany. Its very existence repudiated the East German government's claim to be the legitimate government of all of Germany. Twice (in 1948 and 1958) war had seemed near as the Soviet Union tried to force the west out. In 1961 the Berlin Wall had been built to prevent a mass exodus from East to West Germany. Yet Khrushchev still wished to remove the western presence totally. Also, according to international law, if Cuba was willing to accept these weapons, it was perfectly legitimate to send them.

In 1962 Khrushchev decided to send secretly three MRBM and two IRBM regiments to Cuba—a total of about 80 missiles in all. Also sent were 12 tactical, or battlefield, nuclear missiles, to be used by the Soviet commander, at his own discretion, if the island was invaded. Soviet documents released after the ending of the Cold War also suggest that Khrushchev, always a gambler, felt the need to assert himself in the Kremlin. . . . His only doubt seems to have been that Castro might refuse the missiles, though in fact the Cuban leader accepted them with little hesitation.

The entire project was meant to be kept secret until the missiles were operational. . . .

From Shock to Action

By August 1962 the first rumours of Soviet missiles in Cuba, from émigré reports and CIA [Central Intelligence Agency] leaks, appeared in the US press. Soviet diplomats, unaware of the project, issued flat denials. This made the sense of shock when they were discovered by a U-2 spy plane, on 14 October 1962, even more profound. Kennedy was stunned. He felt Khrushchev's conduct was inexplicably provocative. Khrushchev, in fact, had never considered that the presence of missiles in Cuba would be deemed a monstrous threat in the United States. Nor had he realised that Kennedy and the United States would not tolerate the massive blow to their prestige that would result if the weapons were allowed to remain. In fact the weapons would make very little difference to a strategic balance that was massively in America's favour. But their presence would give the appearance of a weakened America, and in the Cold War appearances were vital. For his part, Kennedy gave no thought to Khrushchev's motives: the missiles had to be removed. . . .

There was an alternative to invasion—a naval blockade of Cuba. . . . This would violate international law, and while it would prevent new weapons arriving, might do little to remove those already on Cuba. But it was a limited and measured response, which would avoid forcing Khrushchev into a corner where he [would] have to fight to avoid utter humiliation. . . .

Only on the 22 October, when the blockade was prepared, was news of the missiles and America's response made public. It caused immense shock in the USA and internationally—it had to, to drown out the Soviet response that they were acting legally and responding in kind to US actions in Turkey. Khrushchev's reply was to bluster that the USSR would assert its rights on the high seas and to accuse Kennedy of bringing the world to the brink of a nuclear catastrophe. . . .

On 23 October, as 27 Soviet ships headed towards the blockade, many carrying military equipment, presumably including missile parts, Kennedy, who had assumed that Khrushchev would back down, had to consider what to do if his blockade was defied. As the world stood on the brink of nuclear war, news reached Kennedy that the first Soviet ships had stopped and turned back.

The Road to Settlement

The crisis was not over. Nuclear missiles remained on Cuba and Kennedy was determined to remove them. A resolution had to be found and quickly. . . . Both leaders, it is clear, had become horrified at the prospects in front of them. Kennedy . . . ordered the navy to allow Soviet and Soviet-chartered merchant ships not carrying arms to pass unsearched. Khrushchev, for his part, sent a long, rambling letter to Kennedy, appealing to reason and trust to prevent a catastrophe, and insisting that if US threats to Cuba were ended, the issue of weapons would disappear. . . .

Khrushchev's message seemed to contain the basis of a settlement. But matters took a turn for the worse. A new message was received from Moscow offering a specific deal by which the missiles in both Turkey and Cuba would be removed and the USA and USSR would jointly guarantee the security of both nations. . . .

Kennedy was interested. It was not an unreasonable deal. . . . In the message to Khrushchev agreed by Excomm [the executive committee of the National Security Council], Kennedy insisted that the missiles in Cuba must be removed and offered to end the blockade and pledged not to invade Cuba if that happened. But when he delivered it to the Soviet ambassador, Kennedy's brother, Robert, added a private message that once this was done, after a few months had passed, the Turkish missiles would be withdrawn. . . .

Khrushchev, himself desperate to find a settlement and aware that a non-invasion pledge would meet his most important need, did agree. Tedious and frustrating negotiations followed over the means of verifying the departure of the missiles, largely caused by the obstruction of Castro, who was enraged that Khrushchev had not consulted him over the settlement.

In the end the Russian ships departed with their hatches uncovered, allowing the Americans to see the missiles leaving. To repay Castro for his awkwardness, Kennedy refused to confirm the pledge not to invade Cuba. In fact, however, it was observed, though small-scale sabotage raids by the CIA continued.

Credit and Blame

Kennedy certainly came out of the crisis with a reputation greatly enhanced in the west. Khrushchev, for his part, was deemed by his colleagues to have suffered a humiliation, and the crisis was one of the issues that led to his being deposed in October 1964.

Certainly once the enormity of the situation became clear to both men, they showed responsible leadership and a determination to find a peaceful resolution. Both rejected hard-line advice and were careful not to escalate the crisis. Khrushchev might even be said to have shown greater courage in making what was publicly seen as the larger concessions.

In the aftermath of the crisis they both worked to improve relations and prevent a recurrence of such a

> Both men had acted recklessly in bringing the crisis about.

confrontation. The 'hotline', allowing direct communication between both leaders, was installed and the Partial Test Ban Treaty of September 1963 signified a first step towards arms controls. Kennedy's hope to build on these steps, brutally ended by his assassination in November 1963, further heightened his statesman-like image.

However, both men had acted recklessly in bringing the crisis about. Khruschev (and Castro) should have realised the dangers of surreptitiously introducing nuclear weapons into Cuba. They could not realistically be kept secret, and the US reaction should have been predictable. Conventional forces, perhaps a couple of Soviet armoured brigades, should have been enough to deter a US invasion of Cuba, without risking a major confrontation. Kennedy, for his part, allowed his vendetta against Castro to overcome good sense. Operation Mongoose [a covert U.S. operation] was hardly the act of a statesman. He also rejected the use of discreet diplomacy. A secret message to Moscow, requiring the quiet removal of the missiles, might have avoided a confrontation, though admittedly giving Khrushchev the chance to prevaricate until the missiles were operational. But perhaps Kennedy felt he had to make a tough stand after the Bay of Pigs, and—though there is no proof of this—he may have had an eye on the impact this would have on the forthcoming Congressional elections.

The Dangers of the Cuban Missile Crisis Were Underestimated

Phillip Knightley and Peter Pringle

In this 1992 British newspaper article, Phillip Knightley and Peter Pringle assert that 30 years later, Cuban, American, and Soviet leaders who took part in the Cuban missile crisis acknowledge that at the time they underestimated the danger. Decision makers and advisers on all sides misinterpreted each other's beliefs, objectives, military strength, and command structures. In actuality, they contend, a low-ranking military officer on either side could have taken an action that would have launched an all-out nuclear war. Phillip Knightley is an Australian-born journalist who has authored numerous books, including *The First Casualty: The War Correspondent as Hero and Myth-Maker from the Crimea to Iraq*. Peter Pringle is a foreign correspondent and the author and coauthor of several nonfiction books.

SOURCE. Phillip Knightley and Peter Pringle, "The Cuban Missile Crisis 1962: The World at Death's Door," *The Independent*, October 5, 1992, second part of article was on October 6, 1992. Copyright © 1992 Independent Newspapers (UK) Ltd. Reproduced by permission of the authors.

Thirty years ago this month [October 1992], the Cuban missile crisis raised the spectre of nuclear war. Photographs taken by an American U-2 spy plane over western Cuba on 14 October revealed a missile launching ramp under construction. [U.S. president] John F Kennedy accused the Soviet leader, Nikita Khrushchev, of planning to put nuclear missiles on the island—100 miles from the American mainland. This was contrary to Khrushchev's assurances that Soviet military aid to the Cuban leader, Fidel Castro, was solely for defense against any US invasion. Kennedy imposed a naval blockade to stop Soviet ships . . . carrying the missiles from reaching Cuba, and prepared to invade the Island. Khrushchev ordered his ships and their submarine escorts to sail straight through the American fleet and told Soviet forces to resist any US landing. Then, at the last minute, Khrushchev backed down, the Soviet ships reversed course, and within weeks all missile sites on Cuba were demolished. The free world hailed President Kennedy as a hero who, in an eyeball-to-eyeball confrontation with the Communists, had made Khrushchev blink. That, in essence, is the received version of the Cuban missile crisis. The truth is even more terrifying.

> The world was actually on the brink of a nuclear holocaust in which the first strikes alone would have wiped out 500 million people.

A Real Danger Underestimated

Those readers who took part in the Cuban missile crisis who are still alive now agree that at the time they greatly underestimated the danger. The world was actually on the brink of a nuclear holocaust in which the first strikes alone would have wiped out 500 million people.

Robert McNamara, then US Secretary of Defense, now says: 'Events were moving out of control.' Georgi Kornienko, an adviser to Nikita Khrushchev, now says:

'We were closer to nuclear catastrophe than we have ever been before or since.' Fidel Castro, who urged Khrushchev to make a pre-emptive nuclear strike on the United States in the middle of negotiations, now says: 'If my position had prevailed, there might have been a terrible war. I was wrong.'

The fact is that all the leaders and their advisers during the missile crisis were guilty of misconstruing the others' beliefs, intentions, determination, military strength and command structures. The crisis developed its own momentum until the danger that all-out nuclear war might be started by a second lieutenant became very real. Our interviews in Washington and Moscow, and information from recently-released archives in both countries, confirm that:

- Soviet nuclear missiles had already arrived in Cuba at the time of the crisis. So had some of their warheads. They could have been made ready for firing within hours.
- The Soviet commanders in Cuba had permission to fire nuclear missiles at an American invading force without first consulting Moscow.
- In 1962, American nuclear missiles in Europe had no safety keys and John Kennedy was seriously worried that a US officer would fire missiles at the Red Army without his permission.
- American Minuteman missiles aimed at the Soviet Union during the crisis were later found to have electronic faults which could have caused them to launch themselves.
- Both leaders feared that if they did not reach agreement quickly they would lose control of the military, who were eager to make the first strike.

With the seconds to Doomsday ticking away, Kennedy and Khrushchev had to communicate by cable—which took eight to ten hours. The Soviet ambassador in Washington, Anatoly Dobrynin, recalls: 'We had to ring up Western Union and a black man on a bicycle would come around.'

Khrushchev's Motives

The mystery of the crisis is: why did Khrushchev initiate it? One theory is that the Cuban revolution aroused a powerful sentiment in die-hard Bolshevik leaders. [Soviet deputy premier] Anastas Mikoyan said: 'We've been waiting all our lives for a country to go Communist without the Red Army. It's happened in Cuba and it makes us feel like boys again.'

Khrushchev's son, Sergei, says that when the Cubans crushed the CIA [Central Intelligence Agency]-sponsored invasion at the Bay of Pigs in April 1961, 'not only the government but the people viewed the Cubans as heroes, being next door to the huge neighbour but having the audacity to disagree with him. We decided that we should give Cuba modern weapons to respond to the next US aggression. . . .'

> If the Soviets had fired nuclear missiles at US troops then America would have replied with an attack on the Soviet Union and a full-scale nuclear war would have followed.

But a more convincing explanation is that Khrushchev was only continuing a policy conceived by [former Soviet leader Josef] Stalin: that every opportunity should be taken to shock the Americans into accepting the Soviet Union as an equal in the nuclear age. This is the view of the Soviet military. . . .

The military plan for stationing the missiles in Cuba was called Operation Anadyr. Devised by General Simeon Ivanov, deputy chief of the Soviet general staff, its details have only recently emerged. It deployed medium-range R-12 missiles and long-range R-14 missiles in various locations scattered around the island. By

the time of the crisis, 36 nuclear warheads were available for these missiles—sufficient to destroy all important American military targets and East Coast cities, along with their inhabitants. . . .

When Khrushchev briefed the man who was to be commander of the Soviet forces in Cuba, General Issa Pliyev, . . . the question arose over who could order the firing of these missiles. The strategic missiles—those

Robert McNamara, secretary of defense during the missile crisis, said in 1992 that the world was closer to nuclear war in 1962 than was widely believed by the participants. (AP Images.)

capable of reaching the US—would remain under the control of the commander-in-chief, Khrushchev. But after some thought Khrushchev gave Pliyev permission to employ the nine tactical Luna missiles for the immediate defence of Cuba in the event of a US invasion. . . .

No one we spoke to doubts that if the Soviets had fired nuclear missiles at US troops then America would have replied with an attack on the Soviet Union and a full-scale nuclear war would have followed. . . .

A fleet of 85 ships was assembled in eight ports in the Baltic, the Black Sea and the Barents Sea. The whole operation was shrouded in secrecy. . . .

The first freighter, the *Maria Ulianov*, arrived in Cuba on 26 July, followed by nine others during the next four days. Weapons and equipment that looked like agricultural goods were unloaded around the clock. Tanks, missiles and special military equipment were unloaded only at night. Soviet troops were sent to their designated areas wearing Cuban army uniforms and all commands were spoken in Spanish.

The Secret Missile Operation Revealed

But it was not possible to keep secret for ever an operation of this size. The use of so many ships from the Soviet merchant fleet meant that there were not enough for normal trade, and the Soviet government had to go to the international charter market to make up the shortfall. In the close-knit shipping world this did not go unnoticed, but the connection with Cuba did not come until August.

In that month, Philippe de Vosjoli, the Washington station chief for the French intelligence service, visited Cuba. It was obvious that there were a lot of Russian troops around: the CIA estimated 10,000, but there were actually 43,000. . . . De Vosjoli collected several reports of missiles being unloaded and transported and he passed on this information to the director of the CIA, John McCone.

On 10 August McCone put together de Vosjoli's information, that from the Cuban exile community in the US, and a list of the movements of Soviet cargo ships from the Black and Baltic seas to Cuba. He concluded that Moscow was up to something new and different in Cuba. His senior officers scoffed at the idea: at worst, they said, the Soviets might be building SAM [surface-to-air] missile sites there. McCone's response was, 'So what are the SAMs meant to protect?' And he came up with his own answer—nuclear missiles. Over the objections of his senior officers, he wrote to Kennedy the same day, voicing his suspicions.

At a National Security Council meeting on 22 August the president brought up McCone's memorandum. Kennedy did not believe that Khrushchev would take such a risk, since the US had 5,000 ballistic missiles to the Soviet Union's 300. But he ordered his defence chiefs to draw up a contingency plan to deal with a situation in which Soviet nuclear missiles were deployed in Cuba.

Meanwhile in Cuba, all was not going well. Attempts to speed up the construction of the launch pads failed because the Soviet troops could not cope with the heat, humidity and mosquitoes. Moscow then decided to send an eight-man delegation of senior officers from the Defence Ministry to supervise the work. . . .

When General [Anatoly] Gribkov, who was to lead the delegation, went for his final briefing, [Soviet defense minister Rodion] Malinovsky repeated Khrushchev's orders about control of the missiles: 'We do not want to unleash an atomic war. That is not in our interests. The missile divisions must only be used with the personal approval of Khrushchev. But the tactical Luna missiles can be used by Pliyev . . . , using his own judgment, in the event of an attack by the US and an imminent landing of troops on the coast. . . .

Soviet Duplicity and an American Warning

Moscow, meanwhile, was putting out a barrage of lies to mislead the Americans. On 4 September, the Soviet ambassador in Washington, Dobrynin, who knew nothing about the missiles, told [U.S. attorney general] Robert Kennedy that Khrushchev had asked him to assure the president that he would not place any offensive missiles in Cuba.

Dobrynin repeated this promise to Theodore Sorensen, the president's speech writer, at lunch two days later. In response to these false assurances, Kennedy now made two major mistakes. First, he stepped up plans for an invasion for Cuba. . . .

These were only contingency plans, and Kennedy later insisted he had no intention of implementing them. But he failed to consider how these preparations would appear to Castro. When the Cuban leader learnt of them from his intelligence service, he naturally concluded that an American invasion was imminent.

Next, at the urging of his brother, Robert, and mainly for domestic political purposes, Kennedy issued a public warning to Khrushchev that if the US ever found 'offensive ground-to-ground missiles' in Cuba, then 'the gravest issues would arise': a statement so precise that it was to leave him with no alternative but a full confrontation with the Soviet Union.

> Kennedy was furious. He told Bundy that Khrushchev 'can't do this to me . . . one way or another, the missiles have to go.'

Photographic Evidence of Soviet Missiles in Cuba

On Sunday 14 October the weather was clear enough to allow a U-2 flight over western Cuba. The film was flown to Washington, and on the morning of Monday 15

October, a team of CIA experts in a National Photographic Interpretation Centre laboratory . . . began to examine it. It was late evening when one of the technicians, hunched over a light-box, called his supervisor to look at a photograph of San Cristobal, 100 miles west of Havana. To a non-expert, the photograph appeared to reveal little of significance (Kennedy said later he wondered why the U-2 had taken photographs of a football pitch). But to an expert, the photograph was a revelation.

One of the intelligence prizes which the Soviet defector Oleg Penkovsky had brought to the West was a Soviet military manual dealing with the construction of missile sites. Like all military machines, the Soviet one did things strictly according to the manual.

By comparing pictures of known intercontinental ballistic missile sites in the Soviet Union with Penkovsky's manual, the CIA had been able to identify what its experts called 'the foot-print' for each type of missile site.

The supervisor looked at the San Cristobal photograph and saw the footprint of a medium-range nuclear missile site, probably an SS-3. He said, 'Don't leave this room. We might be sitting on the biggest story of our time.'

The American Reaction

McGeorge Bundy, the national security adviser, went to the White House the next morning, Tuesday 16 October, and broke the news to the president. . . . Kennedy was furious. He told Bundy that Khrushchev 'can't do this to me . . . one way or another, the missiles have to go.'

At 11.50 A.M. the president chaired a meeting in the Cabinet room at the White House. Those present, the civilian and military leaders of the US, were to become 'ExComm,' the executive committee of the National Security Council. They were to meet . . . almost continuously throughout the crisis.

The dominant feeling at the meeting was shocked surprise. Robert Kennedy later recalled: 'We had been deceived by Khrushchev, but we had also fooled ourselves. The intelligence community, in its national estimate of the future course of events, had advised the president on four occasions that the Russians would not make offensive weapons available to Cuba. The last estimate was dated 19 September and it advised him that, without reservation, the United States Intelligence Board had concluded that the Soviet Union 'would not make Cuba a strategic base'.'

The feeling of the meeting was that some form of action was required and that a surprise air strike against the missiles would be the only course. Listening to the military explain how this could be done, Robert Kennedy passed his brother a note: 'I now know how [Japanese prime minister Hideki] Tojo felt when he was planning Pearl Harbor.'

The Dangers of the Cuban Missile Crisis Have Been Exaggerated

Robert Manning

In the following 1997 editorial, Robert Manning argues that, contrary to a widely held view, the October 1962 Soviet-American confrontation over Soviet missiles in Cuba did not take the world to the brink of nuclear war. U.S. president John F. Kennedy had the edge; the odds that he could force Soviet leader Nikita Khrushchev to withdraw the missiles from Cuba were very much in Kennedy's favor, and Khrushchev knew it. Manning asserts that Khrushchev had no desire—or intention—to push the confrontation to conflict; the risk was too high. Journalist and author Robert Manning served as assistant secretary of state for public affairs from 1961 to 1963 and as editor for the *Atlantic Monthly* magazine from 1966 to 1980.

Thirty-five years have passed since President Kennedy and a dozen of his key advisers deliberated for several suspenseful days how to deal with a brazen power play by the Soviet Union. The "Cuban missile crisis" has gone down in history as the near-meltdown moment of the cold war, the confrontation that took the world to the brink of nuclear war. That apocalyptic view is now firmly fixed in contemporary mythology. But did the two nations really come close to nuclear war? As one who sat in on some of those White House deliberations in the president's cabinet room, I believe that the case can be made that the dangers of that 13-day interlude in October 1962 have been greatly exaggerated.

From the moment the United States discovered that the Soviet missile emplacement was underway, the odds that President Kennedy could face down Nikita Khrushchev and force him to withdraw the weapons were overwhelmingly in Kennedy's favor. This is not just a hindsight conclusion. You need to examine the facts that were available to both sides, either explicitly or implicitly, overtly or subliminally, at the time.

At the outset, Secretary of Defense Robert McNamara and some of the key military men offered assurance that Soviet missiles in Cuba would, as the president's national-security adviser, McGeorge Bundy, reported, "make no decisive difference in the strategic balance." This did not make the missiles in Cuba acceptable, but it surely defined the threat as essentially psychological, a potential blow to America's psyche and a probable inconvenience to future conduct of American foreign policy. Something to worry about, of course. But to go to nuclear war over? Well, that was for Khrushchev to worry about.

The first recommendation of a majority of the president's advisers (the so-called Excomm of the National Security Council) was to blast out the missiles and their emplacements with airstrikes. This plainly implied a mind-set of confidence that such resort to force could be applied with probable impunity; why else would so many responsible men urge it on the reluctant president as the best way to deal with Khrushchev's folly?

The president wondered whether any American action, either an airstrike or blockade, might precipitate yet another Soviet action against the Western presence in Berlin. But it was as evident to the Soviets as to the Americans that any act that sought to depose the West and threatened to set overwhelming Soviet land forces against the 200,000 U.S. and NATO forces in Europe would leave the president with only two alternatives—to surrender those forces or retaliate with nuclear weapons. Could any president surrender in those circumstances? None had more reason to face that question than Khrushchev. And he knew the answer.

> "Khrushchev was . . . a bluffer."

The Soviet Union possessed at that time as few as 75, and no more than 300, strategic missiles. The United States could target and deliver perhaps as many as 5,000 nuclear warheads. To some American theorists this passed for a "parity" of sorts, but surely it could not look like that to Moscow, even without factoring in Soviet paranoia. If Khrushchev were so lunatic as to launch a first strike and kill thousands of Americans, it would be but a terrible prelude to having his country wiped off the face of the earth. "Khrushchev knows that we have a substantial nuclear superiority," McGeorge Bundy was to write later, "but he also knows that we don't really live under fear of his nuclear weapons to the extent he has to live under fear of ours."

Khrushchev was impetuous, bombastic, reckless; he was also a bluffer, as Eisenhower discovered when he faced him down over Berlin in the 1950s. But in my several years of experiences in and out of government

U.S. president Dwight Eisenhower (right) saw Soviet leader Nikita Khrushchev (far left) as a bluffer because of the USSR's response in the 1961 Berlin crisis. (AP Images.)

I never heard anyone, not even CIA analysts, suggest that he was insane. Indeed, in the most crucial of the messages he exchanged with Kennedy during the Cuba confrontation, he said "only lunatics or suicides, who themselves want to perish and to destroy the whole world before they die," would push the confrontation to conflict. "I'm not crazy," he was saying. There was no other way to translate that message except as a plea from a man who knew he'd gone too far. And keep in mind that he was dealing with the one country that had already demonstrated a willingness to use the nuclear weapon against human beings.

It seemed to me during those 13 days, as it does today, that all those factors dictated a peaceful settlement. Of course there was suspense and concern, dramatically documented in the new book "The Kennedy Tapes: Inside the White House During the Cuban Missile Crisis." There can be miscalculation of even the most carefully calculated risk. But was this situation, as favorable as it was to the United States, really more dangerous than the Berlin situation had been for many years? Or the ceaseless circlings of nuclear-loaded SAC bombers [Strategic Air Command] and flotillas of nuclear-armed U.S. and Soviet submarines prowling the seas, when the possibilities of human missteps or twisted communications were numberless?

> Even selfless participants in a dangerous confrontation can come to see it as more threatening than it was, thereby making the defusing of it more heroic.

In the 35 years since, the participants on both sides of the confrontation have continued to say that it was. They have held three conferences at which they exchanged information, traded theories and canonized each other for having saved the world from cremation. At each conclave the mythologizing process has accelerated. At the most recent one in Havana, in 1992, a Russian general went so far as to say that Soviet troops in Cuba had been given authority by Moscow to fire nuclear missiles at the United States if they felt the need to. The general was a pompous windbag, and his claim proved to be patently untrue, but former defense secretary McNamara returned to the mainland to state that we had come "even closer" to nuclear war than he had believed in October of 1962.

Which brings me to Manning's Maxim: Even selfless participants in a dangerous confrontation can come to see it as more threatening than it was, thereby making the defusing of it more heroic.

CHAPTER 3

Personal Narratives

A Reporter Remembers the Cuban Missile Crisis Hitting Close to Home

John Bogert

Photo on previous page: President Kennedy's announcement of the U.S. intention to blockade Cuba stopped many Americans in their tracks. (Jim Mooney/ NY Daily News Archive via Getty Images.)

In the following viewpoint, John Bogert recalls how he felt as a thirteen-year-old living in Florida during the Cuban missile crisis. He explains that even though he knew what was happening was an "international event," he was terrified and could not help taking it personally. He relates what he was told in school about what would happen if the Russians attacked Fort Lauderdale. He goes on to describe the scene close to his home and how what was happening made Floridians feel. He comments on how quickly the crisis ended and tells how things changed when it did. John Bogert is a staff columnist for the Torrance, California, newspaper, *Daily Breeze*.

SOURCE. John Bogert, "For Some, the Cuban Missile Crisis Hit a Little Closer to Home," *Daily Breeze*, October 20, 2002. Copyright © 2002 Los Angeles Newspaper Group. Reproduced by permission.

I like to recall the Cuban missile crisis, a monumental screw-up taking a 40th anniversary bow this week, as the time I nearly died.

Excuse me for having taken an international event so personally. And, yes, I am aware that the near-death of what we laughingly call Western Civilization was not all about me.

Only I didn't know that as a terrified kid facing a tragic end in south Florida, in the easy-out zone of those mid-range Russian missiles.

Not to worry. Worry is for creeps who don't understand tough-guy American foreign policy that is anti-Soviet enough to die for, literally, leaving the living to envy the vaporized.

As my seventh-grade social studies teacher explained, if the Ruskies [Russians] take out the sleepy beach town of Fort Lauderdale, our massive flying arsenal will instantly reduce Russia to an uninhabitable wasteland, making us the winners!

Tomorrow [October 21, 2002] marks the anniversary of that terrible week's beginning, the week we went toe-to-toe with the commies, the week that "The Monster Mash" was a free nation's No. 1 hit single. It should also be noted that the Top 10 TV shows of that mean season all featured cowboys.

Meanwhile, our movie star president was sounding maybe a little fatalistic saying, ". . . the cost of freedom is always high, but Americans have always paid it."

A Lot to Learn and Endure

I was 13 years old and about to pay. But first we had to endure the threats and counter threats. We had to learn what quarantine meant and about target radius and how Cuba somehow got to be 90 miles from Key West, from the very slip where the ring-a-ding-ding crowd used to take the overnight boat to the morals-free Mafia casinos.

There I was some insignificant miles north, hardly embarked upon a life that was about to be snuffed out in a cloud of fissionable material. That material then being under the strict control of two young, scared-stiff Russian officers and a paranoid dictator.

Luckily we still believed that responsible men in suits were in charge of this mess when what was in fact happening was a freak-out at the highest levels. The brass was telling JFK [John Fitzgerald Kennedy, the U.S. president] to hit them hard while JFK, for all I know, was still missing dear departed [movie actress] Marilyn [Monroe].

This while the Russian premier worried not about JFK, but about guys like Gen. Curtis LeMay, a man who spent the previous war demonstrating his willingness to bomb everything.

Experiencing War in Florida

Only this war was an affront to our honor and security.

Which is a noble sounding thing to say until the flatbed trucks start rolling down Federal Highway, one block from my front door, bulging with green-tarped field guns and tanks. While the spot down at Port Everglades where we fished got concertina wired and swarmed with green fatigues.

> To the residents of low rent paradise, this was the Florida War, the week our hurricane and bug-plagued world became D-Day England.

This as submarines sat lethal and gray, lashed six deep along the sea walls as carrier battle groups idled where the blue line of the Gulf Stream met a momentarily mushroom-cloudless sky.

To the world, this was all about Cuba. To the residents of low rent paradise, this was the Florida War, the week our hurricane and bug-plagued world became D-Day England.

This was war's terrible uncertainty come to our streets while mom shopped the Piggly Wiggly for glass bottles of orange soda meant to sustain us after bombs fried the atmosphere.

That's another thing that has come to light. The Russian lads in Cuba had authority to use short-range nukes on our massed invasion fleet. They were prepared, as one of them later put it, to inflict ". . . horrendous casualties."

Including him. Including me.

And even if we survived I knew what to expect: giant ants, mutant spiders and me kissing Barbara Heitzenrater as the doomsday cloud floated our way on a tropical breeze.

Then it ended. No more terror, no more crowding into a sweat-stinking junior high cafetorium to hear our president say "Cuber." The whole insane event was suddenly over, defused as quickly as it had begun with life, good old life, quickly slipping back into its normal fear of total annihilation—leaving the backyard shelters never used and Barbara Heitzenrater never kissed, not by me, except in dreams.

A British Journalist Recollects the Two Weeks of the Missile Crisis

Peregrine Worsthorne

In the following viewpoint, Peregrine Worsthorne tells why the two weeks of October 1962 were extraordinary and, for people like him who lived through it, more than a crisis. He describes the general sense of disbelief experienced when U.S. president John F. Kennedy announced that there were Soviet missiles in Cuba and that the Soviets refused to remove them. He tells of the hushed mood he experienced in Washington, D.C., during his visit there and paints a vivid picture of the influential guests at a dinner party he attended. Peregrine Worsthorne is a British journalist, writer, and broadcaster.

SOURCE. Peregrine Worsthorne, "Kennedy's Finest Hour," *Spectator*, October 19, 2002. Copyright © 2002 by The Spectator. Reproduced by permission of *The Spectator*.

Forty years ago, the Americans won what I hope will be the nearest thing to nuclear war between superpowers—of which only one is left—ever fought; and the fact that they won it without firing a shot should not diminish but rather increase the extent of the victory.

What I am referring to is known, of course, as the Cuban Missile Crisis, which is how it will go down in history. But for those of us who lived through that extraordinary fortnight in October 1962, it was more than a crisis. First, the placing of Soviet nuclear missiles in Cuba, within 90 miles of the American coast, was an explicit and unequivocal *casus belli* [event used to provoke a war]; as explicit and unequivocal as would have been the placing of American nuclear missiles in [former leader Josip Broz] Tito's anti-Soviet Yugoslavia. What followed was a fortnight of bloodless battle in which nuclear armed missiles were deployed by both sides—with the Russian commanders, at least, free to use them—and finally a Russian surrender when her ships carrying nuclear reinforcements to Cuba were threatened with force by the American navy and air force unless they turned back. So if thermonuclear war can be defined as the confrontational deployment of thermonuclear weapons to alter the balance of power, then that is, indeed, what did take place. It was not unlike one of those mediaeval conflicts when opposing armies rushed about making lots of noise without actually being joined in battle.

A State of War Between East and West
Almost from the moment President Kennedy announced to the world the discovery of the Soviet missiles in Cuba, to the moment he announced that [Soviet] first secretary [Nikita] Khrushchev had agreed to withdraw them, a state of war, to all intents and purposes, existed between East and West. We did not expect the sirens to start sounding, as they had after [British prime minister

> Surely Mr Khrushchev could not be so mad as to have done something which, unless reversed, was bound to lead to a thermonuclear exchange between superpowers.

Neville] Chamberlain's announcement of war in 1939, but that was only because we knew full well that on this occasion there would be no time for them to sound. I say almost, since for a day or two we simply did not believe that President Kennedy was telling the truth. His surveillance people, we wildly surmised, must have made a mistake. Surely Mr Khrushchev could not be so mad as to have done something which, unless reversed, was bound to lead to a thermonuclear exchange between superpowers—i.e., to the end of civilisation.

Even these scant grounds for hope evaporated, however, when Dean Acheson, that most distinguished of all American secretaries of state, visited London and Paris with the photographic proof-positive; and it was after seeing them that I flew to Washington to report on what we all thought might well be not so much the war to end war as the war to end everything. How does one say goodbye to one's family on such a mission? For once the old phrase 'too awful to think about' was genuinely applicable, and we did not think about it . . . much.

A Time of Tense Excitement

In those days the *Telegraph* allowed us to travel first class, and on the flight to Washington I sat next to the young and already famous Australian singer Shirley Abicair, who was due to give a concert in New York. We talked all night, even held hands; and my heart still gives a jump whenever I hear one of her songs. There was no question of sleep. Ever since Hiroshima [site of U.S. atomic bombing of Japan], the mushroom cloud had been a nightmarish possibility hanging over all our imaginations, and now, quite suddenly, it was threatening to materialise. Oddly enough, fear did not come into it, so there was no need to keep a stiff upper lip; no need to 'eat, drink and be merry, for tomorrow we die.' For if everybody was going to die, then nobody was going to die, since dying involves leaving loved ones behind and this time there were going to be no loved ones left behind. No need, therefore, for tears or sadness. It was more a question of intense excitement; of being in on not the creation but the destruction of the world; in on, that is, the drama to end all dramas.

> " The total public silence from the White House had succeeded in communicating determination more effectively than any number of official communiques. "

The atmosphere in Washington, when we arrived, was extraordinarily subdued. From the moment of announcing the exclusion zone, President Kennedy and his small team of advisers had gone into purdah [isolation] in the White House, making no appearances and issuing no statements. This unprecedented hush lasted for several days during which there was nothing much to do except wait and pray and hope for the best. I think we all knew by then that if anybody was going to flinch from this eyeball-to-eyeball confrontation, it would not be President Kennedy. How we knew that I do not know, but we did, and somehow or other the total public silence from the White House had succeeded in communicating determination more effectively than any number of official communiques.

I had arranged to stay with old friends, Phil and Sherry Geyerlin. He was then in charge of the editorial page of the *Washington Post* and a friend of Kennedy's. But even a well-connected journalist such as Phil had no idea what was going on. Then came the sensational newsflash: the Soviet ships had turned back. We all began to breathe again.

A Prestigious Dinner Party

Weeks before the crisis, however, Phil and Sherry had arranged a dinner party, all thought of which had been expunged from their minds if only because two of the guests—the brothers McGeorge and Bill Bundy—were part of the presidential team that had been immured in the White House. At about 6.30 P.M. on the day the crisis ended, I was sitting with Phil in his study when the telephone rang. It was McGeorge Bundy himself calling from the White House. He just wanted to make sure, he said, quite matter-of-factly, that he and his brother Bill were still expected for dinner.

And what a memorable dinner it turned out to be. In style it was overwhelmingly patrician Wasp [white Anglo-Saxon Protestant]. In spite of, or perhaps because of, being Catholic-Irish, President Kennedy liked to surround himself with members of the Wasp patriciate—or, if not actual members of that traditional governing class, their co-opted honorary ethnic-minority members who, in their dress, manners and accents had become indistinguishable from it—one of whose principal characteristics, very much like that of Britain's old ruling class, was to take for granted that their place was centre-stage when great national events unfolded. Most of the company had known each other since birth, and been at the same schools and universities. They sat happily round the table, mulling over the history-making events of the previous two weeks, differentiating the hawks from the doves, etc., much as the Duke of Wellington's commanders might have done when dining together after the defeat of Napoleon at Waterloo.

> I shall never forget being in Washington during Kennedy's finest hour.

Kennedy's Finest Hour

The next day, the President, who had been secluded during the crisis, held a special press conference, opening it with the memorable phrase 'Long time no see.' It was a theatrical occasion, and, as I put it in my star-struck dispatch to the Sunday *Telegraph*, 'Before the crisis he had been the glamorous Prince Hal; now he was every inch King Henry V.' Very little of what came to be known as the myth of Camelot has survived, but I shall never forget being in Washington during Kennedy's finest hour, when it really did seem to make sense for an Englishman—or at any rate for this Englishman—to want to march to the American drum.

But that was 40 years ago, when Jack Kennedy had just outstared and outwitted the rival superpower, and thereby won for himself the right to act like the Emperor of the West, without a shot being fired. Wisely, however, he did not go on to demand a change of regime in the Soviet Union, in spite of its leader having willfully and insanely brought the world to the brink of thermonuclear conflict.

Peregrine Worsthorne calls the Cuban missile crisis President Kennedy's finest hour, although he was let down by the remainder of Kennedy's time in office. (AP Images.)

Shortly thereafter, of course, Kennedy went on to use American power to try unsuccessfully to overthrow Ho Chi Minh, the North Vietnamese dictator, whose crimes against his own people and the threats he posed to his neighbours in South-East Asia did seem to make him a worthy enemy of mankind. It was a doomed adventure, which made my generation averse for evermore to accepting any other American president as Emperor of the West.

All this, I repeat, was 40 years ago: old history. But history, as we know, can repeat itself: the first time as tragedy, then as farce. Well, belonging to the generation that survived the tragedy, who are we to fear mere farce?

A Soviet Naval Officer Goes to Battle over Cuba

Vadim Orlov

In the following viewpoint, Vadim Orlov talks about his experiences on the Soviet submarine B-59 during the Cuban missile crisis. He explains that he was a commander of one of the Special Assignment Groups (OSNAZ) assigned for the first time in Soviet naval history to boats going to Cuba. He describes the welcome his group received and the crowded conditions onboard the vessel. He tells how the vessel tried to escape discovery by anti-submarine forces and what happened when it reached the Sargasso Sea and was no longer able to avoid its opponents. Vadim Orlov served as a communications intelligence officer and commanded the Special Assignment Group on the Soviet submarine B-59 during the Cuban missile crisis.

SOURCE. "The Cuban Samba of the Quartet of Foxtrots: Soviet Submarines in the Caribbean Crisis of 1962," *Military Parade Magazine*, Moscow, 2002. Translated from Russian to English by Svetlana Savranskaya. Reproduced by permission.

*T*he crew of B-59, under the command of Second Captain Valentin Savitsky . . . had to drink the cup of hardships to the bottom. Many things happened on that trip: the diesel coolers got blocked with salt, rubber sealing got torn, and the electric compressors broke. When in the vicinity of Cuba, in the evening, the boat came to the surface to charge the accumulators, American anti-submarine aircraft appeared in the sky. They had to submerge urgently. But the charge in the accumulators was practically zero.

Let us give the floor to the witness of the events—Second Captain Retired [Vadim] Orlov, who was Commander of Special Assignment Group (OSNAZ) on submarine B-59. . . .

Even before the Cuban Mission of the 69th Brigade, submarines conducted intelligence gathering on autonomous missions. . . . However, it was conducted on so to speak handy means. As a rule, the boats were not equipped with special equipment, and the available radio technicians were engaged in the interception of the radio signals of the potential enemy. For the first time in the Soviet naval practice, special OSNAZ groups were assigned to the boats, which went to Cuba, and they received special equipment. We were all young specialists, who just completed the courses of retraining for signals intelligence several months ago. When they selected us for the OSNAZ, it appears that they took into account my good knowledge of English. Because it is not enough to intercept a communication, one has to understand it.

> "I cannot say that we received a good welcome in the 69th Brigade."

The OSNAZ: From Rejection to Respect

I cannot say that we received a good welcome in the 69th Brigade. Preparing for the length of the planned

A Soviet submarine surfaces in an unidentified body of water. Amid trying circumstances that included depth charges exploding near his vessel, Soviet sailor Vadim Orlov and his fellow submariners resisted retaliating against the U.S. Navy. (AFP/Getty Images.)

trip, the boats had to take additional food reserves, and those were stored in compartments. The officers of the Brigade Headquarters were also on the boats. In other words, even without us, the ships suffered from lack of room and overpopulation. And there we were, with all our equipment. We also needed separate rooms. In addition, the OSNAZ groups were not small. The group of B-59 consisted of 9 people. This "excess" [of people] was due to the fact that some of our specialists were supposed to establish ground posts of signals intelligence in Cuba. In short, when I turned up on the board of B-59, Second Captain Valentin Grigorievich Savitsky upon reading the instructions, in which it was said, in particular, that the OSNAZ groups [were] supposed to ensure security of the submarine for the length of the mission, muttered angrily. . . . "It's interesting—how are you going to ensure our security?" His reaction is understandable. An experienced submariner, he saw a green youth in front of him, a 25-year-old Senior Lieutenant, who had never been on a submarine on an autonomous mission before. It was only later, when we started to produce reliable reports about the actions of the NATO [North Atlantic Treaty

Organization] anti-submarine forces that the attitude toward us began to change—from rejection—sometimes even sharply negative—to respect.

> **It felt like you were sitting in a metal barrel, which somebody is constantly blasting with a sledgehammer.**

Encounter with the Enemy

The anti-submarine forces of the opponent, especially the aviation, were ready for an encounter with us from the very beginning of our sail to the Cuban shores. And even though myself and other commanders of the OSNAZ groups knew about the goals and the route of our mission, without which it would have been impossible to plan and carry out our work, we could not have expected this kind of counteraction [by the opponent]. In the beginning, the Norwegian hydroplanes were searching for us, then at the Farer line—the British "Shackletons." Then it was the turn of the American "Neptunes." But judging by the events, they had not succeeded in discovering us. In any case, not until we reached the Sargasso Sea. There they got us. A naval forward-searching aircraft carrier group headed by the aircraft carrier "Randolph" confronted submarine B-59. According to our hydro-acoustic specialists, 14 surface units were following our boat. Together with the navigator, we did parallel plotting [on the map]—he did the route of B-59, as he was assigned; I recalled my first naval specialization—and plotted the movements of the American ships. For some time we were able to avoid them quite successfully. However, the Americans were not dilettantes [rookies] either—following all the canons of the military art, they surrounded us and started to tighten the circle, practicing attacks and dropping depth charges. They exploded right next to the hull. It felt like you were sitting in a metal barrel, which somebody is constantly blasting with a sledgehammer. The situation was quite unusual, if not to say shocking—for the crew.

Withstanding the Attack

The accumulators on B-59 were discharged to the state of water, only emergency light was functioning. The temperature in the compartments was 45–50 C [113°–122°F], up to 60 C [140°F] in the engine compartment. It was unbearably stuffy. The level of CO_2 [carbon dioxide] in the air reached a critical practically deadly for people mark. One [of] the duty officers fainted and fell down. Then another one followed, then the third one. . . . They were falling like dominoes. But we were still holding on, trying to escape. We were suffering like this for about four hours. The Americans hit us with something stronger than the grenades [depth charges]—apparently with a practical depth bomb. We thought—that's it—the end. After this attack, the totally exhausted Savitsky, who in addition to everything, was not able to establish connection with the General Staff, became furious. He summoned the officer who was assigned to the nuclear torpedo, and ordered him to assemble it to battle readiness. "Maybe the war has already started up there, while we are doing summersaults here"—screamed emotional Valentin Grigorievich, trying to justify his order. "We're going to blast them now! We will die, but we will sink them all—we will not disgrace our Navy!" But we did not fire the nuclear torpedo—Savitsky was able to rein in his wrath. After consulting with Second Captain Vasili Alexandrovich Arkhipov . . . and Deputy political officer Ivan Semenovich Maslennikov, he made the decision to come to the surface. We gave an echo locator signal, which in international navigation rules means that "the submarine is coming to the surface." Our pursuers slowed down.

U.S. Airmen Serve in Puerto Rico During the Missile Crisis

Louis A. Arana-Barradas

In the following viewpoint, Louis A. Arana-Barradas describes the Cuban missile crisis as a scary time for those stationed at Ramey Air Force Base near Aguadilla, Puerto Rico. Three servicemen who served at the base during the crisis share their experiences and their thoughts about life on and near the base during the two weeks of the crisis. They describe ways in which the base changed and what it was like to be unsure how serious the situation really was. Louis A. Arana-Barradas is a master sergeant in the U.S. Air Force and an editor of *Airman* magazine at the U.S. Air Force News Agency.

The United States and Soviet Union were staring each other down at the time. Playing a deadly game of chicken. Both had their fingers on

---

SOURCE. Master Sgt. Louis A. Arana-Barradas, "On the Brink of Doom," *Airman*, October 2001, pp. 22–27.

the launch buttons of their nuclear missile arsenals. One twitch and they'd plunge the world into a nuclear holocaust. . . .

At Ramey Air Force Base [Aguadilla, Puerto Rico], Capt. Rafael Marquez was on alert again. Nothing new for the Strategic Air Command KC-135 pilot. For a week, he lived in an alert facility next to the base flight line. And each day he sat in the sweltering refueling jet for up to six hours. And for each of those minutes, he hoped he wouldn't have to launch.

"We waited for 'the balloon to go up' so we could scramble," he said.

In his patrol truck, Staff Sgt. Arturo Morales made his rounds of the base. Driving down the nearly deserted streets, the air policeman knew this was the real deal. This wasn't just another SAC [Strategic Air Command] exercise cooked up to spoil his evening.

On the road next to the flight line, he passed foxholes filled with soldiers. Antiaircraft gun batteries stood at the ready. Sentries and their dogs were on patrol around the clock. Visible in the faint moonlight was a sight the cop remembers to this day. The parking ramps were crammed with B-52 Stratofortress bombers and tankers as far as he could see.

Ramey sits on high cliffs overlooking the Atlantic Ocean. It was an assignment for which airmen fought. Cooled by tropical breezes, its golf course was legendary in the Air Force. As were its white sandy beaches.

Now miles of barbed wire shrouded its picturesque beauty. Ramey was an armed camp.

"We were ready for anything anybody could throw at us," Morales said.

'Everyone wondered what tomorrow would bring.'

A Scary Time

About a mile from the base, Jose "Quique" Suarez sat in a rocking chair on his porch. The evening breeze rustled the "Flamboyan" trees in his front yard. A civilian accountant at Ramey, he could hear the rumble of jets taking off on another mission.

Life at the base continued. But things were different. People stayed close to home. . . .

"Everyone wondered what tomorrow would bring." Suarez said.

It was a scary time, October 1962. The events that took place that month—known as the Cuban Missile Crisis—brought the world to the brink of doom—Armageddon. . . .

The people of the world held their collective breaths and waited to see what would happen. Fidel Castro mobilized Cuba. And U.S. forces went on full alert.

At Ramey, some 600 miles east of Cuba, the four men wondered what would happen to their families. They knew the Soviets had aimed some of the missiles at Ramey. So they wondered if Soviet missiles would vaporize their dreams while they slept.

Details of what was going on were sketchy, Suarez said. Base leaders didn't provide much information. He said it was to avoid a panic. But to report "there was a problem" didn't help matters. It only fueled rumors.

"There was no CNN back then," he said. "We relied on what we were told. So we thought things would surely happen somewhere else. Nobody thought Ramey would be involved."

But it was. Soon more aircraft joined the base's 72nd Bomb Wing. The alert facilities filled up. And there were a lot of drills.

"We knew that any time we launched it could be for real," Marquez said. Bomber and tanker crews had less than 10 minutes to launch once an alarm sounded.

As the crisis continued, people got a lot of information by "reading between the lines" of what officials were saying, said Suarez. . . . Still none of the men thought events would escalate to war.

Besides, on an island often hit by hurricanes, he said, waiting out the crisis was like riding out one of the big tropical storms. Some people did expect the worse—that missiles would destroy the base—and sent their families home to the States, or elsewhere.

Doubts About a War

"I tried not to listen to that stuff, but it was hard not to," said Morales, who was also born and raised in Aguadilla. "I didn't think the Russians would be stupid enough to launch missiles. So I concentrated on my work—12 hour shifts without a break—and didn't think about it."

Marquez is from San Juan, the Puerto Rican capital. His wife was expecting their fourth child at the time. She was eight months pregnant, and he worried about her. More so than the situation he was facing. He didn't think there would be a war.

"We were talking about Cuba, here," he said. "Nobody thought the Russians would get involved, risk going to war, over Cuba. But we were highly trained and ready in case they did." . . .

"We were all in this together," [Airman 3rd Class Michael Kud-Kudjaroff] said. "It was us against them." He, too, didn't think there would be a war. But he did have one worry.

"I hoped some young airman like me—with his finger on the launch button—wouldn't say, 'What the hell, let's see what happens if I push this button,'" he said.

> 'Nobody thought the Russians would get involved, risk going to war, over Cuba.'

Trying to Cope

As the days ticked off, there were more drills at the base. School kids dove under their desks when the alarms went off to recall airmen who lived off base. Bomber and tanker crews not on alert continued to fly missions—some as far away as Spain. People stocked up on canned goods and filled containers with water. The only people who could enter the base were those who worked there. And base residents didn't leave.

Everyone waited. To keep people's minds off what was going on, base services outlets stayed open longer. Sporting events picked up. So did events for families.

But in Aguadilla and other towns, rumors spread fast. Many Puerto Ricans thought Ramey would be bombed, Suarez said.

"People were telling others not to take jobs on the base. To avoid it like the plague," he said.

And so people from other parts of the island made excuses not to visit their relatives who lived near or on base. The rumors made things tough on base, too. Because with the little information base officials were releasing, believing rumors was easy to do, he said.

Suarez and Morales, who lived off base, had to answer for the Air Force when their neighbors and friends asked them what was going on.

"I explained as much as I knew, which wasn't much," Morales said.

> 'I sometimes still feel the tension we felt standing alert here that October.'

Suarez, whose father helped build Ramey in 1939, told family and friends what base people were doing to cope. Soon, many Puerto Ricans started doing the same things.

"They stayed away from the beaches, tried to stay calm and waited," he said.

There were some things Suarez didn't tell family and friends. Like he overheard a young pilot tell a friend before he went on alert: "Good-bye, I don't know if I'll ever see you again." Or that a pilot friend asked him to take care of his family should he not make it back from a mission.

"That's when I realized the situation was more serious than I thought," he said. . . .

An End to the Crisis

Then on Oct. 28 "Khrushchev blinked," as historians put it. Backed down. He agreed to dismantle the missiles in Cuba. . . .

The crisis was over. And the world let out a sigh of relief.

Kud-Kudjaroff was probably the happiest airman in Puerto Rico. Off alert, he and his pals headed for their squadron club in the barracks where they lived. He put a nickel in the jukebox and tossed back a few cold ones. Nobody wanted to talk about what had just happened.

"I had a lot of catching up to do," he said. "I was missing my girl, good movies, steak and lobster, and rum and Cokes."

Suarez, Marquez, and Morales went back to their families. All of them tried to analyze what they'd just lived through. But they had no answers. They were just glad it was over. . . .

Thirty-nine years after the close call, the veterans meet at annual reunions of the Ramey Air Force Base Historical Association. They sometimes talk about those two critical weeks in October. Only now they see things differently. That they were a blink away from nuclear war.

"What I've come to realize most is that the people who were not close to the base were more scared than we were," said Suarez, who still lives in the same house.

Marquez lives outside the base, too. He drives by the old alert ramp each day on his way home. Surprisingly, the crisis brings back fond memories of how he loved to serve in SAC. It was a tough outfit, but more so on the families than the crews, he said.

"I sometimes still feel the tension we felt standing alert here that October. And not knowing if we would scramble off to war," he said. "I'm glad we crossed our fingers and nothing happened."

The youngest of the bunch, Kud-Kudjaroff now lives in Tucson, Ariz. He didn't take the events of that October seriously until later in his life. Now he realizes how naive he was about the power of nuclear weapons. But so were most Americans then.

He doesn't know if Kennedy or Khrushchev—or both—prevented the war. That debate will go on forever, he said. Today he realizes that all it would have taken to start a fight was for someone to panic. That, he said, "is a really scary thought."

"If the Cuban Missile Crisis did anything," he said, "it made the world grow up."

A U.S. Naval Officer Helps Photograph Soviet Missiles

Peter A. Huchthausen

In the following viewpoint, Peter A. Huchthausen describes his experiences as an assistant communications officer on the USS *Blandy* during the Cuban missile crisis. He details the roles he and other crew members played as everyone worked together to fulfill their mission to track and intercept Soviet vessels leaving Cuba and photograph their deck cargo—missiles in particular. He describes encounters with two Soviet merchant ships and paints a vivid picture of the difficulties he and the other members of the *Blandy*'s intelligence photo team endured trying to fulfill their mission. Peter A. Huchthausen served on the USS *Blandy* during the 1962 Cuban blockade. He was a historian and the author of nine books.

SOURCE. Peter A. Huchthausen, *October Fury*. Hoboken, NJ: John Wiley & Sons, Inc., 2002. Copyright © 2002 by Peter Huchthausen. All rights reserved. This material is used by permission of John Wiley & Sons, Inc.

After escorting [Soviet] Captain [Nikolai] Shumkov's B-130 [submarine] for the night and into the daylight hours, we passed the contact to USS *Keppler* and departed at twenty-five knots to check one of the first merchants [ships] departing Cuba under the conditions of the new agreement with the Soviet Union. We had been ordered to join the forces assigned to intercept and track Soviet merchant ships departing Cuba. . . . That last Sunday morning, October 28 [1962], the Soviet government had announced on the air that they would withdraw their missiles from Cuba.

Blandy became one of dozens of U.S. destroyers sent to intercept designated Soviet merchantmen removing military equipment and personnel from Cuba. The mission called for the destroyers to come close enough to the merchant ship to be in good camera range and photograph the deck cargo; the most immediately important were the medium- and intermediate-range ballistic missiles. . . . The air of the presence of the Soviet troops and equipment on the ground in Cuba was so blatantly underhanded, the military had been required to wear civilian clothing, which they did, ironically with the traditional blue-and-white-striped, long-sleeved jersey under their tropical shirts. But it certainly wasn't difficult to tell the Russians or the Ukrainians, with their high cheekbones and ski jump noses, from the swarthy Cubans.

The first merchant ship we intercepted was the Soviet-flagged dry cargo ship *Dvinogorsk*, a ten-thousand-ton freighter from Odessa with a deckload apparently of the SS-4 missiles. A helicopter from the carrier *Essex* delivered a photographer's mate to us from the Combat Camera Detachment at Atlantic Fleet headquarters. The photo mate, a young third-class petty officer barely nineteen years old, arrived on the fantail looking pale and frightened with a sophisticated camera and a huge telephoto lens to ensure that we obtained top-quality photos.

Preparations for the Missions

With a fresh mission in hand, our XO [executive officer], Lieutenant Commander Lou Lester, was catapulted into action, briskly organizing a special action bill for the new assignment. In the navy the shipboard bill is used as the organizational basis for life itself. All activity is keyed to a written chart, called a bill, which assigns every man a place and a function for every activity. . . .

Aboard *Blandy* there was a watch quarter and station bill, ASW [anti-submarine warfare] action bill, replenishment bill, abandon ship bill, boarding party bill, dress-ship bill, and cheer-ship bill, plus now a count-the-missiles bill. . . .

During preparations for this mission, not more than a few hundred miles northeast of Havana, at the height of an international crisis, the XO's tireless efforts unearthed a Russian-speaker aboard. The linguist was a naturalized U.S. citizen named Walter Dubicki, originally from Czechoslovakia, who spoke native Czech and some Ukrainian in addition to some Russian. Dubicki was the classic sailor, a second-class petty officer, machinist's mate from the repair division who had been on destroyers in Newport for decades. . . .

As assistant communications officer working under instruction with Bill Morgan [the combat information center watch officer], I was responsible for preparing signals to send by flashing light to the Russian ships, directing them to a specific course and speed. I worked with Petty Officer Dubicki to get the signals right in simple English so he could put them into phonetic Russian. . . .

Getting in Place to Take Photos

As we steamed toward the first missile-carrying merchant ship, we rehearsed the new bill. Since the exec had suddenly designated me as the ship's collateral duty intelligence officer, I was put in charge of getting the new photo mate eighty feet up the mast to perch with me on the air search radar antenna platform, to take photos when alongside the Soviet merchant ship. We planned to photograph each of the missiles as it was uncovered and then forward the film and the accompanying intelligence report by helicopter to the carrier for forwarding onward to Atlantic Fleet headquarters as quickly as possible.

Blandy moved in close to the merchant ship *Dvinogorsk* from astern after a long, six-hour chase and signaled her by flashing light in international Morse, in English and Russian, the required phrases from the new operation order: "Please steer course zero six zero degrees true, at twelve knots, and begin uncovering your missiles for inspection, in accordance with the agreement between our two countries."

> The newly designated intelligence photo team, consisting of the frightened photo mate and me, climbed up the solid steel rungs welded permanently to the mast.

The newly designated intelligence photo team, consisting of the frightened photo mate and me, climbed up the solid steel rungs welded permanently to the mast. I improvised a knapsack to carry the large box camera, lenses, film, and sound-powered phone set. A slight sea was running, with two-to-three-foot waves. Eighty feet up the mast, however, these were magnified in intensity so that it took all my strength and concentration to haul the camera gear and to coax the reluctant photo mate while holding on for dear life. We secured ourselves to the mast with safety straps, and I donned the sound-powered phones and watched. Happily, the weather was fair, since we were within a hundred miles of Havana, and the wind, although at that height strong, blew warmly.

Dvinogorsk complied with the flashing light signal and came slowly to the required heading and speed. There was a long delay as our signalmen sent and resent the directions to uncover the forward missile port side.

Four canvas-covered missiles were arrayed on the ship's main weather deck. There were also about five hundred Soviet soldiers in khaki uniforms lounging at the rails on several levels, peering at us as we inched ever closer. The Russians began slowly to comply and, while sitting quietly high up the mast, I noticed, to my dismay, that the photo mate was apparently suffering terribly from vertigo and beginning to turn green. He motioned to me suddenly that he was going to be sick; and while unable to do anything to help him because of the violent pitching and rolling, I hung on and watched helplessly as he literally blew his breakfast to the winds. As the poor sailor retched repeatedly, I worried that if events did not move more quickly he would be too weak to hold the large camera.

Slowly the topside Soviet soldiers on the merchant ship went below-decks, and a working party of five deckhands and a large bosun mate set about uncovering the first missile. I helped position the ship by adding and reducing revolutions by phone to the bridge watch and got the photographer's mate ready. With the application of some soda crackers and an orange, which I had brought from the wardroom, the photo mate was able to stop heaving. Later, on a second run of this same evolution, I passed him some seasick pills, but these, too, also left him after a short stay. Nonetheless, we repeated this routine until we had obtained detailed photos of each missile uncovered and, with the photographer's mate in a much weakened state, descended the mast during a long break to clear up some problem we were having with the Russians.

Uncovering the Missiles

During the long period alongside *Dvinogorsk*, Commodore Charles Morrison had been in constant conversation with the task group commander aboard *Essex*. While I was up on the mast with the photo mate, I wondered about the long delays between times when the Russian crew uncovered one of the four missiles on deck and before we were told to take the photos. The issue arose over the presence of the inside rubber casing that wrapped each missile tightly. The missiles were encased in this rubber shielding presumably to protect them from the weather. As *Blandy* flashed over to the freighter . . . to uncover the missiles, the Russian deck force team would proceed to the missile and take off the outer canvas wrap and stand back so we could observe and shoot a photo. But that wasn't good enough for Captain [Ed] Kelley.

> 'How the hell do we know there are missiles under those casings and not some gigantic sausage, Commodore?'

"How the hell do we know there are missiles under those casings and not some gigantic sausage, Commodore?"

"Ed, we were told to direct them only to uncover their missiles. What do you think is inside?"

"I think we should send [Les] Westerman and his team over to open the entire casing and have the combat cameraman shoot the damn things close up," Kelley roared. "How the hell else can we be certain?"

Captain Kelley's insistence had caused great furor aboard the carrier; the admiral kept repeating the question. "Can you verify that those are missiles?"

"Of course I can't verify those are missiles, Commodore, until I have Westerman go aboard and touch them." . . .

Waiting to Resolve the Issue of the Missiles

Eventually Commodore Morrison sent the same answer back to the task group commander in *Essex* in a long flashing-light message. Then came an inordinately long delay. I remained on the mast with the seasick photo mate. The commodore called for a meeting of his staff to discuss the issue, the OOD [Officer of the Deck] drove the ship out to a safer distance of about a hundred feet from *Dvinogorsk*, and the XO huddled with [caterer] Stonewall Jackson, planning how to feed the crew while standing extended hours at special sea detail for refueling. But we weren't refueling, and there was no such drill in the books, and Jackson was adamant that we wait until we finished and then he would serve everyone at the regular mess. But the exec insisted . . . we had already been alongside the stubborn Russian for two hours. And it looked as if we were to remain alongside until the issue was solved.

Apparently the issue went all the way to [the] Atlantic Fleet commander in chief in Norfolk and to the defense secretary and the White House. At question was whether the Russians were complying with the recent agreement to submit to inspection by U.S. ships to ensure that they were removing their missiles from Cuba. Ed Kelley's stubbornness in insisting that the Russians open the inner seals was sticking in the craw of the agreement. . . .

> That was the first in a series of *Blandy*'s encounters with Soviet merchant ships, and probably one of the most exciting.

Finally Captain Kelley drafted a message describing the issue succinctly. . . . Kelley described the missiles when we were alongside *Dvinogorsk*:

About sixty feet long and four feet in diameter. Apparently missiles without nose cone attached. Appears to check with unclassified photos MRBM [medium-range ballistic missile]. Small tarp removed. Skin-tight canvas tailored to fit not removed. Four stubby canard stabilizing fins noted. Bulge of wiring conduit visible . . . although outer cover removed, and outline of objects appeared to correspond with

MRBM, fact that objects remain covered with tailored cloth makes positive identification of objects as missile problematical. . . .

This message was sent to the commander in chief of the Atlantic Fleet from the ASW group commander in USS *Essex*, although originally drafted by Captain Ed Kelley.

The problem was finally addressed in the Pentagon. . . .

Meanwhile, I remained atop the mast, and Steve Jackson had been ordered to conduct battle messing, which meant feeding the crew on extended sea detail stations. We all ate baloney sandwiches on station with coffee—that is, all who weren't aloft on the mast. I was finally called down and handed two sandwiches by Stonewall, and happily was able to eat both, eight feet up on the SPS-6 air search radar platform, since it was doubtful the seasick photo mate could hold down anything more than the few saltines and orange he had already consumed.

The Episode of the Fizik Kurchatov

That was the first in a series of *Blandy's* encounters with Soviet merchant ships, and probably one of the most exciting. We were sent to check a second, called *Fizik Kurchatov*. This time we thought we had the procedure down, but things never go the way they are planned. I was standing the eight-to-twelve watch on the bridge with Gary Lagere. It was initially a quiet watch following a day that had been tense and full of surprises.

We sighted *Fizik Kurchatov* and found her steaming northeast at twenty knots. That put us in a long stern chase, but we finally pulled alongside at first light the next morning. We repeated our signal, "Your government has agreed to uncover missiles. Please do so beginning on the starboard side, number one missile."

Again we repeated the drill. This time the seas were running from the north, and a good wind was blowing. As we went alongside at refueling distance, I stood poised on the 04 level above the pilothouse on the Mark 56 Director deck waiting for the signal to go aloft. As I stood there watching the Soviet ship as we made our approach at about fifty feet, I noticed that the main deck of the Soviet merchant was full of troops who wore khaki trousers and blue-and-white T-shirts. They were standing observing us just as our crew were, at least those not busy on a sea detail station. We sent over the distance line, which they understood and handled as if they had done the drill before. As we were jockeying for position and transmitting the signals to uncover the missiles, a hatch on the side of the *Kurchatov* superstructure burst open and a female emerged, who took one step over the hatch coaming [raised framework]. Apparently surprised to see a U.S. warship at such close range, she poised, startled. As she stood there, a gust of wind suddenly blew her yellow skirt up, which enshrouded her head and revealed a comely pair of legs and finely turned ankles. A loud roar and applause erupted on the inboard side of *Blandy* as the poor lady struggled to pull her skirt down to cover herself. The Russians, too, when seeing the American reaction, applauded loudly. At that moment I wondered what we were really doing here, and all fear of the other side seemed to vanish. They were pretty much like we were.

Two Cubans Share Their View of the Missile Crisis

Alexander Denton

In the following viewpoint, Alexander Denton focuses on the recollections and views of his grandfather, David Lopez, and his great aunt, Melva Amorín, both of whom lived in Cuba during the 1962 missile crisis. They both had strong anti-Castro and anti-Soviet leanings. They affirm that the Soviet Union plan to place missiles in Cuba was kept secret from the Cuban people and describe how they finally found out what was happening. They both express their belief that the only thing the Cuban government gained from the crisis was an agreement that the United States would not invade Cuba. Alexander Denton is a student in Boulder, Colorado, and a 2008 first-place winner in the Junior Web Site category of the Colorado History Day contest sponsored by the University of Colorado in Denver.

SOURCE. Alexander Denton, David Lopez, and Melva Amorín, "The Cuban View: The View From the Island: My Family Lived in Cuba During the Crisis," Telephone Interview with David Lopez, February 2, 2008, and Telephone Interview with Melva Amorín, February 3, 2008, www.alexanderdenton.net, 2008. Reproduced by permission of the author.

These are the accounts of two people that lived in Cuba during the Missile Crisis.

David Lopez, my grandfather, . . . lived in the country near the town of Morón. On the other hand my great-aunt Melva Amorín . . . was living in Havana, Cuba. Neither of them agreed with the regime; they both had and have very anti-Castro and anti-Soviet Union views. . . .

David Lopez

I know the October Crisis of 1962 as the Soviet's intent to submit the United States to their will. To achieve this goal the Soviet Union planned to place large range missiles, nuclear and non-nuclear, in strategic places throughout Cuba and to aim them at the United States.

Since this was a secret mission, the Cuban government kept it hidden from the Cuban population. We would see big trucks with radar and other heavy equipment traveling on main and back roads between the cities of Morón and Ciego de Avila in the province of Camagüey and not know what the mission was. It felt weird that there was such heavy equipment movement in the area, but we had no official word on what was going on.

> The October Crisis brought fear, confusion and uncertainty to those of us who knew what was truly happening.

Our family found out about the crisis through La Voz de los Estados Unidos de América [The Voice of the United States], a clandestine radio station that transmitted from the US to Cuba in short wave and that we listened to in hiding. We then realized that the big trucks that were transporting heavy equipment near our farm were related to the missile base that was being built in the area.

This conflict was started by the Soviet Union in collaboration with [Cuban revolutionary leader] Fidel Castro who had declared himself and the country "communist" and had declared the great hatred that he had towards the United States.

The missile bases were uncovered by the pictures taken by reconnaissance airplanes sent by the United States to Cuba. Since one of the missile bases was close to where we lived, we got to see some of those planes fly over our house. They flew relatively low and made a lot of noise. Those were scary times.

In my opinion, the truth is that President [John F.] Kennedy was very skillful in winning this conflict with the Soviet Union. The United States prevailed over the Russians in this conflict since they forced the Soviets to abort their plan to arm Cuba against the United States and the rest of the Western Hemisphere. The Russians wanted to be the "Great World Power" but they failed. What Cuba and [Soviet] President [Nikita] Khrushchev got out of the conflict was Kennedy's promise to not invade Cuba.

To enforce the agreement, President Kennedy used the naval power of this great nation to impose a naval block-ade on the island thus preventing Russian ships loaded with nuclear cargo from arriving in Cuba. The American Marines inspected and returned all 18 ships that were in transit to Cuba back to the Soviet Union. This news was very welcome to us, the Cubans who did not agree with the Castro regime. It brought us great happiness to see that Castro had failed in his attempt to side with the Russians and submit the United States to the Soviet's will.

The October Crisis brought fear, confusion and uncertainty to those of us who knew what was truly hap-pening. It also brought great relief to see that it had been resolved with the United States prevailing. However, we understood that the Cuban people were going to pay a price long term as the American-Russian agreement left no room for the United States to intervene in Cuba ever again. We were now on our own.

Compromise solved the conflict.

Melva Amorín

In April of 1962, well-trained and armed young Cuban men who were living abroad tried to invade Cuba with the intention of liberating it from the tyrannical government established the 1st of January 1959. Unfortunately this mission failed.

It was six months later when Cuba, allied with the Soviet Union, decided to build military bases all over the Cuban territory for large-scale missiles that Russia would provide with the purpose of attacking the United States.

It was then when we realized that we were threatened with an imminent war of unprecedented consequences for us Cubans.

I knew what was going on because I listened to the short-wave radio transmissions of a US-based radio station La Voz de los Estados Unidos de América. The Cuban government prohibited this, but we would listen to it at night and in hiding.

In the end, and before the threat became reality, the United States was victorious while Russia was defeated. Russia was not able to install the missile bases aimed at destroying the United States of America in Cuba. This strategy would have made Russia the number one super power in the World.

The only advantage that the Cuban government got out of it was the agreement between Mr. Khrushchev and President Kennedy that the United States could not invade Cuba.

GLOSSARY

Bay of Pigs	Unsuccessful attempt in 1961 by U.S.-backed Cuban exiles to overthrow the Cuban government of Fidel Castro.
Bolsheviks	Revolutionaries who, under the leadership of Vladimir Lenin, formed the Russian Communist Party in 1918 and began calling themselves Communists.
Camelot	Term used to describe the presidency of John F. Kennedy.
CENTO (Central Treaty Organization)	Organization formed in 1955 by Iran, Iraq, Pakistan, Turkey, and the United Kingdom.
CIA (Central Intelligence Agency)	Independent U.S. government agency responsible for collecting and coordinating intelligence and counterintelligence activities overseas in the national interest.
Cold War	Attempt after World War II by the Soviet Union and the United States to gain world influence by means short of total war.
ExComm (Executive Committee of the National Security Council)	Group of advisers assembled by U.S. president John F. Kennedy during the Cuban missile crisis.
glasnost	Soviet government cultural and social policy of the late 1980s that encouraged open discussion of political and social issues and freer distribution of news and information.
ICBM (Intercontinental Ballistic Missile)	Missile that follows a ballistic trajectory and has the range to carry a nuclear bomb about 3,400 miles.
IRBM (Intermediate-Range Ballistic Missile)	Ballistic missile with a range of a few hundred miles to 1,500 miles.

Jupiter	Intermediate-range ballistic missile.
Kremlin	Seat of the Soviet government from 1918 until the dissolution of the Soviet Union in 1991.
Marxism-Leninism	Official political theory of the former Soviet Union.
MRBM (Medium-Range Ballistic Missile)	Ballistic missile with a range of about 1,800 to 3,400 miles.
NATO (North Atlantic Treaty Organization)	International organization created in 1949 by twenty-six North American and European countries to safeguard the freedom and security of its member countries.
OAS (Organization of American States)	Alliance formed in 1948 by the United States and other western hemisphere republics to encourage military, economic, social, and cultural cooperation among member states.
Operation Anadyr	Soviet military plan for stationing missiles in Cuba.
Operation Mongoose	Secret CIA-backed U.S. operation intended to upset the Cuban government and economic infrastructure and totally undermine Fidel Castro.
SAM	Surface-to-air missile.
U-2	U.S. Air Force reconnaissance plane.
USSR (Union of Soviet Socialist Republics)	Soviet state made up of fifteen constituent or union republics in eastern Europe and northern Asia; also known as the Soviet Union.
Warsaw Pact	Treaty signed in 1955 between Albania, Bulgaria, East Czechoslovakia, Germany, Hungary, Poland, Romania, and the Soviet Union creating an organized military.

1959   Fidel Castro takes power in Cuba.

1960   Cuba aligns itself with the Soviet Union and its policies.

1961   The United States terminates diplomatic relations with Cuba; Cuban exiles backed by the U.S. Central Intelligence Agency (CIA) unsuccessfully invade the Bay of Pigs; the CIA begins Operation Mongoose; U.S. president John F. Kennedy and Soviet premier Nikita Khrushchev hold summit talks in Vienna.

April 1962   Premier Khrushchev decides to place missiles in Cuba.

May 1962   A high-level Soviet delegation arrives secretly in Havana to suggest nuclear weapons be placed in Cuba.

July 1962   Soviet ships begin ferrying missiles, troops, and military supplies to Cuba; the United States monitors Soviet shipping activity.

August 1962   A U.S. reconnaissance flight over Cuba reveals the presence of missiles in Cuba.

September 1962   The Soviet ambassador assures the U.S. attorney general that no offensive missiles will be placed in Cuba; the first two shipments of Soviet surface-to-surface medium-range ballistic missiles (MRBMs) arrive in Cuba; the Soviet foreign minister tells the United Nations that a U.S. attack on Cuba or Cuban-bound ships would mean war.

October 14, 1962	An American U-2 plane flying over western Cuba spots and photographs missile sites.
October 15, 1962	Analysts at the National Interpretation Center identify missiles in Cuba as MRBMs.
October 16, 1962	President Kennedy is notified about the missiles in Cuba and calls together a team of advisers to serve as the Executive Committee of the National Security Council (ExComm) to plan what should be done.
October 17, 1962	Premier Khrushchev tells President Kennedy that no surface-to-surface missiles would be sent to Cuba; new U-2 flights reveal additional MRBM sites in varying stages of construction.
October 18, 1962	The Soviet foreign minister assures President Kennedy that Soviet aid to Cuba is strictly for defensive purposes.
October 21, 1962	President Kennedy decides on a quarantine of Cuba as a first action to remove the offensive missiles from Cuba; a U-2 flight reveals the assembly of MIG fighters, bombers, and more missiles on the north shore of Cuba.
October 22, 1962	President Kennedy sends the first of a series of letters to Khrushchev; Kennedy addresses the nation and the world and reveals the crisis and his course of plan for the blockade and quarantine; Fidel Castro announces a general mobilization and war alert throughout Cuba; U.S. military forces go to high alert.
October 23, 1962	President Kennedy authorizes a naval quarantine of Cuba; the Soviet Union requests a meeting of the UN Security Council.
October 24, 1962	The naval quarantine begins, leading some Soviet ships

to reverse course; construction on missile sites in Cuba speeds up; diplomatic efforts continue at the United Nations.

October 25, 1962   The U.S. ambassador to the United Nations challenges the Soviet ambassador to admit that the Soviet missiles exist in Cuba; UN secretary-general U Thant proposes a temporary halt in the actions of both sides; a Soviet ship headed for Cuba is boarded and inspected; American journalist Walter Lippmann suggests a Cuba-Turkey missile trade; Castro authorizes air-defense forces to fire on all American aircraft within range.

October 26, 1962   Premier Khrushchev offers to remove Soviet missiles from Cuba if the United States publicly states it never would invade Cuba; in a private letter to President Kennedy, Premier Khrushchev proposes a peaceful solution to the crisis; the U.S. attorney general meets secretly with the Soviet ambassador and suggests a Cuban-Turkish missile trade, indicating that Turkey must not be a part of any public agreement to end the crisis.

October 27, 1962   Premier Khrushchev demands that the United States also remove its missiles from Turkey; an American U-3 reconnaissance plane is shot down over Cuba, killing the pilot; President Kennedy tells Premier Khrushchev he will accept the October 26 proposals and tells the attorney general to let the Soviet ambassador know that the Turkey missiles are not part of the deal.

October 28, 1962   Premier Khrushchev agrees to withdraw the missiles; Cuban troops take up positions around the Soviet nuclear missile sites.

October 30, 1962   Premier Khrushchev sends a letter to Fidel Castro explaining why he was not consulted before the decision was made to remove the missiles from Cuba.

November 1962   All missiles and bomber aircraft are removed from Cuba; President Kennedy officially ends the quarantine; U.S. forces return to normal peacetime alert levels.

FOR FURTHER READING

Books

Tomas Diez Acosta, *October 1962: The 'Missile' Crisis as Seen from Cuba*. New York: Pathfinder Press, 2002.

James C. Blight and David A. Welch, *On the Brink: Americans and Soviets Reexamine the Cuban Missile Crisis*. New York: Hill and Wang, 1989.

Fidel Castro and Ignacio Ramonet, *Fidel Castro: My Life*. New York: Scribner, 2006.

Peter Chrisp, *The Cuban Missile Crisis*. Milwaukee, WI: World Almanac Library, 2002.

Michael Dobbs, *One Minute to Midnight: Kennedy, Khrushchev, and Castro on the Brink of Nuclear War*. New York: Alfred A. Knopf, 2008.

Thomas Fensch, ed., *Top Secret: The Kennedy-Khrushchev Letters*. The Woodlands, TX: New Century Books, 2002.

Norman H. Finkelstein, *Thirteen Days/Ninety Miles: The Cuban Missile Crisis*. New York: Julian Messner, 1994.

Aleksandr Fursenko and Timothy Naftali, *"One Hell of a Gamble": Khrushchev, Castro, and Kennedy, 1958–1964*. New York: W.W. Norton, 1997.

Alice L. George, *Awaiting Armageddon: How Americans Faced the Cuban Missile Crisis*. Chapel Hill, NC: University of North Carolina Press, 2003.

Howard Jones, *The Bay of Pigs*. Oxford, UK: Oxford University Press, 2008.

Robert F. Kennedy, *Thirteen Days: A Memoir of the Cuban Missile Crisis*. New York: W.W. Norton, 1969.

Carlos Lechuga, *In the Eye of the Storm: Castro, Khrushchev, Kennedy and the Missile Crisis.* Melbourne, Australia: Ocean Press, 1995.

Carlos Lechuga, *Cuba and the Missile Crisis.* New York: Ocean Press, 2002.

William J. Medland, *The Cuban Missile Crisis of 1962: Needless or Necessary?* New York: Praeger, 1988.

James A. Nathan, *Anatomy of the Cuban Missile Crisis.* Westport, CT: Greenwood Press, 2000.

Norman Polmar and John D. Gresham, *Defcon-2: Standing on the Brink of Nuclear War During the Cuban Missile Crisis.* Hoboken, NJ: Wiley, 2006.

L.V. Scott, *Macmillan, Kennedy, and the Cuban Missile Crisis.* UK: Palgrave, 1999.

Sheldon M. Stern, *The Week the World Stood Still: Inside the Secret Cuban Missile Crisis.* Stanford, CA: Stanford University Press, 2005.

Robert Weisbrot, *Maximum Danger: Kennedy, the Missiles, and the Crisis of American Confidence.* Chicago: Ivan R. Dee, 2001.

Mark J. White, *Missiles in Cuba: Kennedy, Khrushchev, Castro and the 1962 Crisis.* Chicago: Ivan R. Dee, 1997.

Periodicals

Adam Bernstein, "Navy Pilot Proved Soviets Had Missiles in Cuba," *Washington Post*, November 13, 2009.

Richard Bernstein, "Meeting Sheds New Light on Cuban Missile Crisis," *New York Times*, October 14, 1987.

James G. Blight, Joseph S. Nye, Jr., and David A. Welch, "The Cuban Missile Crisis," *Foreign Affairs*, Fall 1987.

Robert Dallak, "JFK v. The Dogs of War as the World Held its Breath," *Times*, August 27, 2003.

Michael Dobbs, "Cool Crisis Management? It's a Myth. Ask JFK," *Washington Post*, June 22, 2008.

Brian Dooley, "The Cuban Missile Crisis—30 Years On," *History Today*, October 1992.

A. Walter Dorn and Robert Pauk, "Unsung Mediator: U Thant and the Cuban Missile Crisis," *Diplomatic History*, April 2009.

Max Frankel, "Learning from the Missile Crisis: What Really Happened on Those Thirteen Fateful Days in October," *Smithsonian*, October 2002.

Warren Kozak, "The Missiles of October," *Wall Street Journal*, October 31, 2009.

Peter Kross, "Inside the Cuban Missile Crisis," *Military History*, November 2006.

Sara Lipka, "A Near Miss," *Atlantic*, October 22, 2008.

Robert Pear, "The Cuba Missile Crisis: Kennedy Left a Loophole," *New York Times*, January 7, 1992.

Pierre Salinger, "Gaps in the Cuban Missile Crisis Story," *New York Times*, February 5, 1989.

Sheldon M. Stern, "The Inside Story of the Cuban Missile Crisis Forty Years After the United States Went to the Brink of Nuclear War, The First Comprehensive Narrative Assembled from Secret White House Tapes Shows How President John F. Kennedy Defied the Hawks and Avoided a Conflagration," *Boston Globe*, October 6, 2002.

Sheldon M. Stern, "What JFK Really Said," *Atlantic*, May 2000.

Time, "Essay: The Lessons of the Cuban Missile Crisis," September 27, 1982.

Tim Weiner, "Word for Word/The Cuban Missile Crisis; When the World Stood on Edge and Nobody Died Beautifully," *New York Times*, October 13, 2002.

Web Sites

Cuban Missile Crisis, 1962: The 40th Anniversary (www .gwu.edu/~nsarchiv/nsa/cuba_mis_cri). This Web site, from the National Security Archive at George Washington University, provides declassified documents and other information about the Cuban missile crisis, including photographs, audio clips, submarine naval charts, a chronology, analyses, and materials from the 2002 40th Anniversary Conference held in Havana, Cuba and links to related news articles and publications.

JFK in History: Cuban Missile Crisis (www.jfklibrary.org/ Historical+Resources/JFK+in+History/Cuban+Missile +Crisis.htm). This Web site offers text and recordings focusing on the Cuban missile crisis, its resolution and its aftermath, as well as a link to a related exhibit.

Thirteen Days and History (www.cubanmissilecrisis.org). This Web site includes an introduction to and comments on the movie *Thirteen Days* starring Kevin Costner, primary source excerpts and resource references on lessons of the Cuban missile crisis, and information on nuclear danger today.

INDEX